From
PARENT

Proverbs 22:6
Train up a child in the way he should
go: and when he is old, he will not
depart from it.

II Timothy 1:7
> *For God hath not given us the Spirit of fear; but of <u>Power</u> and of <u>Love</u>, and of a <u>Sound Mind.</u>*

By **Phyllis Austin**

From Parent to Power
2nd edition
Copyright ©2004, 2007 by Phyllis Austin

Austin Reprographics
P.O. Box 361298
Decatur, GA 30036-1298

Editor: Marcy Hicks
Illustrator (Cover) : Gerald Williams

Library of Congress Catalog Control Number: 2006900984

ISBN 978-0-9759917-1-8

Printed in the United States of America

Contact Author:

Email: paustin@parentsthepower.com

Additional books can be ordered online at
WWW.PARENTSTHEPOWER.COM

Contributing to the
Austin
Legacy

Dedications:

To my mother, Gazella Cooper, for instilling in me *that the only boundaries on me are those that I place on myself.*

To my father, Rev. George Cooper, for showing me entrepreneurship.

Acknowledgements:

First and foremost, I give GOD the glory for his grace, love, and vision.

I thank my husband, Demetrius Austin, for providing endless support.

I thank my children for their spirits.

I thank a host of family, friends, colleagues, and associates in the manifestation of this vision.

CONTENTS

Foreword

As a former administrator and teacher, it has been an honor to serve children and parents with *'good values and behaviors'*. To see the spark in the eyes of students who wanted to learn was a daily blessing. I have witnessed parents who have supported and facilitated their child's scholastic achievements, regardless of their economic circumstances.

I have enlightened parents, and they have enlightened me. I have enjoyed working with and learning from parents. We have exchanged information and strategically blueprinted plans to enhance the intellectual accomplishments of their child. Throughout the years, I have been able to compile this data and share it with others to create more successful students and young intelligent scholars.

I remember when one of my former young intelligent scholars returned to visit me. This particular young lady had challenged me from the first day she entered my class as a senior. I was fair, treated students with respect, and had very strict rules and procedures, but this student wanted to do things her way. For example, she would turn in assignments late, and argue and debate about the scope of the assignments. When that did not work, she would try to negotiate. When that failed, she would state, "I'm going to tell my parents." Her parents, however, never contacted me.

Even after this type of student-teacher relationship, she arrived at my door with a huge smile on her face several months after graduating from high school. She was very friendly and nice. I was not surprised; I feel more appreciated once students attend college. We spoke for a while, and she followed me around the class as I worked with the students.

The seniors in my current class were inquiring about college, dorm life, etc. I probed her about college, and she mentioned that everything was just fine. She also added, "I have to tell you something."

She said,

> I don't want to be rude or disrespectful, but you know you used to get on my nerves. Here we were seniors, and you had us doing major assignments - Fetal Tissue research assignments involving medical issues, ethics, and the law... looking up state and federal laws, using LexisNexis, and writing reports.
>
> Anyway, one day I was sitting in lecture, and the professor started talking

about Fetal Tissue research. I couldn't believe that he initiated dialogue about this topic! There were only a few of us able to discuss Fetal Tissue research. However, I was the only one who could respond to the issues of laws and ethics. The professor asked me, "Where did you learn the information?" I said, "In my Human Anatomy and Physiology class. We had to do a medical, ethics, and law assignment on Fetal Tissue Research and Euthanasia." He continued by asking, "Did you attend a private school?" I replied, "No." Subsequently, he inquired as to where I was from and where I had gone to school.

For me, an educator, this story is another Badge of Honor. This story is just one reason why teachers TEACH.

♥♥♥♥♥♥♥

In contrast to parents and students with *'good values and behaviors'*, I have observed parents and students with such poor principles and practices that they have caused the deterioration of learning environments within classrooms. Unfortunately, these parents have a tendency to believe that failing grades, disciplinary consequences (such as in-school and out-of-school suspensions), and mandatory parent conferences are all a part of teachers and administrators being in 'cahoots' with one another,

11

because they do not like their child.

♥♥♥♥♥♥♥♥

A few years ago, a judge suggested that I observe some juvenile trials, and I did. This opportunity allowed me to witness, first hand, how children and parental habits hinder the success of children. At that point, in my professional career, I believed nothing would surprise me about the demeanor of children and parents. I saw a lot: the good, the bad, and the ugly.

It was only until I was an administrator in an alternative school setting, where inappropriate and costly behaviors flourished, did I realize the need for parents to accept their role in the retardation of their child's academic career, the underdevelopment of their child's unique talents, and the prevention of their child from reaching his/her full potential. Seeing this constant and consistent detrimental behavior had me praying every hour of every day. I would ask God, "How do you want me to help these children?" He would answer, "Love and see only love."

The first and last chapters of this book are dedicated to one of the most powerful, uplifting, educating forces in the Universe: *Love*.

♥♥♥♥♥♥♥♥

The purpose of this book is to open the eyes of parents, guardians, and caretakers to the ethics modeled in the home. The people charged with caring for children must first admit to their own behaviors. Only then, can they change any negative actions. In essence, negative behavior will hinder a child's success and positive behavior will enhance a child's success.

In a classroom, students perform to the levels of a teacher's expectations and standards. In a classroom, a teacher may have many different expectations of students. Yes, it is true; a teacher may have similar outlooks for all students or have higher expectations for some, and lower expectations for others. Therefore, as a parent, you are responsible for monitoring your child's teachers' expectations and standards, along with your child's academic progress. Parents, you can do this by communicating with your child, your child's teachers, and school administrators.

In school, students' successes start with their perceptions of society and their place and worth in it. Accordingly, one of your roles as a parent is to open up society to your child. Parents, you can do this by responsibly exposing your child to society: its cultures, attractions, museums, people, opportunities, professions, successes, challenges, and natural environments. Next, you must recognize your child's individual uniqueness and help your child develop a plan to succeed in life.

Table 1

Preparation	Positioning	Opportunities
Knowledge	Right place	Accessing
Skills	Right time	Creating
Ability		
Information		
Equipment/tools		

In life, success is based on three elements: preparation, positioning, and opportunities (Refer to table 1). The person who is better prepared and positioned will have a greater probability of accessing and creating opportunities that lead to success. Such individuals are more likely to prosper in life. The ability to create opportunities requires a set of unique skills: believing in one's self, investing in one's self, strategizing, and conquering the fears of failure and success. These skills must be taught to children. *These skills are not taught in school.* It is imperative for parents to cultivate their child's spirit, nurture their child's self-esteem, protect their child's value, and teach their child common sense strategies for winning and succeeding in life.

One of my mother's favorite sayings taught me about conquering the fear of people:

'*They can't walk on water.*'

A child's perception of society has to be one of being able to access opportunities and see limitless possibilities. Parents, your child must realize that a *valuable, common sense means* of accessing opportunities is achieved through preparation and positioning. You want your child to absorb the importance of school in the preparation, positioning, and opportunity processes. Your child must be able to comprehend the relationship between school and success. Educators will tell you, students who grasp the correlation between school and success do better in school.

♥♥♥♥♥♥♥

In general, this book will focus on unlocking your child's full potential, cultivating your child's uniqueness, and helping your child to be more successful in school. Children whose parents are positively involved in their world are children who are empowered.

Parents, you are the Power behind your Child's Success.

♥♥♥♥♥♥♥

During my fifteen plus years in education, many parents have asked me, "What is the most effective way to help my child?" Whether your child is in public or private school, or if your child has special needs, there are some definite dos and don'ts. This book is meant to serve as a guide to parents.

For over 15 years, 180 days a year, and 7.5 hours every day, I have been around 1000+ kids. Yes, 1000 plus kids each and every day. I have witnessed good behavior, bad behavior, drama, and trauma. I have seen emotional outburst and inward withdrawal. Moreover, in middle and high schools, students' hormones are raging.

Parents, what if every child in a class was like your child?'

Think about it.

♥♥♥♥♥♥♥

In this book, real case scenarios are used to accent the importance of demonstrating appropriate loving behaviors and assist the parent with developing strategies. These real case scenarios allow the reader to enter into the experiences of others.

> My mother has a saying,
>
> *'Be wise and learn from the experiences of others.'*

I truly want you to learn from what others have experienced. Remember, I am on the other side of your actions and your child's responses.

♥♥♥♥♥♥♥

This book is going to make you think about values and choices. You may begin to question your value system and your decision-making skills. You will begin to re-establish your value system or create one. The transference of values and priorities to your child will no longer be assumed.

As a parent, guardian, or caretaker, you will walk away with the ability to demonstrate the manners that you want your child to model. There should never be a case of undemonstrated knowledge and understanding. When you know better, you do better, and you act in a dignified manner.

♥♥♥♥♥♥♥

Parents, there is one point I want to make clear - strive to be a good parent, not a perfect parent. At the end of the day, you want to be able to look at yourself in the mirror, and know that you have done the best you could without excuses. If you cannot do this, you need to rethink and revise your strategy.

The plethora of information presented in this book will help you discover your child's uniqueness and play a positive role in your child's education. In addition, the information in this book will enable your child to reach his/her full potential. Lastly, your child's learning potential, analytical skills, and thinking capacity will be enhanced as you begin to practice the strategies discussed in this book.

As you read this book, take notes.

Let us get started. You will need paper and pen (or pencil).

Parents, you are Power behind your Child's Success.

Introduction

I am honored that you have an interest in this book. To parents, guardians, and caretakers, this book has been designed to help you identify and cultivate your child's uniqueness, develop your child's full potential, and help your child succeed in school and in life. It is because of this design that all parents and all children will benefit from the information presented in this book. Children, who are doing well, will do even better, and children who are not doing well, will do much better.

Parents, you will learn about learning styles, multiple intelligences, and Bloom's taxonomy. You will be able to recognize quality teaching, grade inflation, high and low standards, high and low expectations, and teacher apathy. You will be able to communicate more effectively with teachers to insure a quality education for your child. You will be capable of helping your child learn, and you will be empowered with the knowledge and skills to help your child reach his/her full potential and succeed in life.

Parents, you are the architects of your child.

♥♥♥♥♥♥♥♥

As a community, we must work together to make sure that each and every student has the opportunity to learn in a safe, quality learning environment. I want your child to be in a safe, quality learning environment. I want parents to know the signs of low expectations, low standards, and an unruly class environment. Parents, your child should not be in a learning environment that fosters low expectations and poor classroom management.

To the parents, guardians, and caretakers of children who cause classroom distractions: *It is time to take responsibility for your child.* It is time to stop making excuses for your child's behavior. It is time to **start** demonstrating relentlessly and without ceasing good conduct, which your child needs to display in order to succeed in life. Therefore, this book will teach parenting skills that work in bringing out the best in your child and increasing your child's school performance.

Schools are not requesting much in asking for a safe, quality learning environment. Generally speaking, schools want children to behave properly for about seven hours a day. The classroom setting, in fact, may require less time. For example, middle and high school schedules usually have six 60-minute classes, thereby averaging 360 minutes (6 hours) per day. Therefore, it is unacceptable for a child to act so *'off the chain'* that he/she does not express God given common sense to behave appropriately during school hours.

Think, parents.

♥♥♥♥♥♥♥♥

Let us continue.

Let us examine our first real case scenario. This situation reinforces the adverse effects of the mother's negative behavior and the beneficial effects of the father's positive behavior.

Real case scenario #1

A mother and father have contrasting views on the abilities of their child. The mother has used the excuse that the child is ADHD. However, the first time this matter was brought to the teacher's attention was after third quarter grades were given. The mother sat in a meeting, arguing as to why her child should not have received a 'D'. The father, on the other hand, stated that the child could do better regardless of being diagnosed with ADHD. In addition, he felt that the child was doing much better prior to the diagnosis. After the meeting, arrangements were made for the student to remain after school for tutoring. Although the mother was not comfortable with the decision, she concurred.

The student stayed for tutoring. The teacher noticed the child's due diligence in doing his work - quality work. One day, without notification, the mother entered the room. The mother was quite surprised that the child was working by himself. After the mother left, the child muttered, "I wish she would leave me alone." The teacher, surprised by this outburst, asked why he would make such a comment. The child replied, "I can do the work. I was used to my mother making excuses for me, and so, I just didn't do anything. I settled for average grades until you gave me a 'D' and weren't going to change it."

Sensing something from the statement, the teacher asked, "Is there an incentive for increasing your grade?"   He answered, "Yes, my father will give me a car."

Needless to say, the child earned the grade and got the car.

♥♥♥♥♥♥♥♥

A much more overt picture is outlined in real case scenario #2. It divulges the kinds of activities we do not want. It also confirms how poor parental behavior at home influences poor child behavior at school.

Real case scenario #2

A student gets into a fight. When the altercation stops, the student is yelling and screaming that a teacher grabbed him. As a result, the parent has to attend a mandatory conference before the student can return to school. During the conference, the student, once again, repeats that the teacher grabbed him. Upon hearing this accusation, the parent begins shouting and yelling that the teacher had no right to grab her child.

The administrator concludes that the teacher properly restrained the student to break up the fight. At the end of the meeting, he asks the parent, "Did you think your child was going to stop fighting on his own?" There is no response from the parent. The administrator continues, "Your child's behavior has contributed to his retention in the ninth grade for two years, and he is on track to be retained a third year. "

♥♥♥♥♥♥♥

Parents, who is your child modeling?

Think.

The next real case scenario shines a light on the effects of negative parental interactions, and how refraining from negative interactions can positively affect a child's education.

Real case scenario #3
A couple's decision to have the mother stay at home creates a financial strain on the family. There is much tension in the home. The mother and father air their grievances in front of their daughter, yelling and screaming at one another.

The mother begins to detect some problems the child is having in school. The mother engages in a supportive role. She communicates her concerns to the teacher, and for more than a month, the child receives extra tutoring and supplemental assignments. However, in spite of these efforts, there is very little improvement in the child's work.

At home, the bickering reaches a breaking point. The mother schedules a marriage counseling session. The mother and father are committed to making their marriage work.

Within a week, the parents stop their abusive actions towards one another. Two weeks later, the child's grades dramatically improve.

♥♥♥♥♥♥♥

Parents, throughout this book are real case scenarios about real people and their real experiences. You may identify with these scenarios. You may see yourself in these scenarios. This is good. Only then, will you recognize opportunities to demonstrate more appropriate and loving behavior.

Parents, you are the Power behind your Child's Success.

PART I

PARENTS, GET INVOLVED

1

Exhibiting a loving behavior

Love is defined as a deep affection, devotion. Love is a powerful force in the universe. There are five types of love:

1. Epithumia Love – Physical Desire
2. Eros Love – Romance
3. Storge Love – Natural Affection
4. Phileo Love – Cherished Friendship
5. Agape Love – Unconditional Love

Agape Love

Epithumia, eros, storge, and phileo love require the sense or feeling of affection, passion. However, Agape love is unconditional. It is Agape love that operates by choosing to love, choosing to be loving towards others.

Many people will seek love and seek to love based on their feelings. However, there are fewer people who know the true power of Agape love, loving another individual unreservedly and without expectations. Agape love requires a greater spiritual understanding, because Agape love represents the love God has for us. Agape love is a choice, not a feeling, and God has chosen to love us - unconditionally.

One can choose to love all the time, regardless of feelings, motivations, or other emotions. When one practices this type of love, one is demonstrating Agape love. Agape love is the type of love that parents must practice with their children. There may be moments when you may feel like you do not love your child. Nonetheless, love means fidelity. You must always have the loyalty to exhibit love and the commitment to act lovingly towards your child.

As parents, guardians, and caretakers, you have been entrusted to love your children, for they are in your care. Your children need the proper guidance, support, and protection that can only enter when you love, and they are loved.

Love for your child dictates that you establish values, guidelines, and limits. Love for your child teaches your child right from wrong. Love for your child means disciplining your child with understanding. Love for your child means providing shelter and food for your child. Love for your child means taking your child to the doctor when he/she is sick. *Family love heals.* Love for your child brings you home. Love for your child prevents you from degrading your child with curse words and negative actions. Love for your child protects your child from being abused by boyfriends, uncles, mothers, or fathers. *Again, your innate love for your child protects your child, and it eliminates harmful elements and people from your child's environment.*

Parents, do you honestly love your child?

Think.

I will not judge your answer, and I do not want you to judge your answer. If you answered yes, that is good. If you answered no, that is honest.

Parents, I want you to confess your honesty.

Irrespective of your answer, I want you to choose to love your child with Agape love. I want you to sense love for your child. I want you to choose to love your child and conduct yourself responsibly, whether you want to or not. When you choose to love your child, you are saying that there are no excuses for not loving your child and acting lovingly towards your child.

In deciding to love your child, I want you to operate lovingly towards your child. Your thoughts, your behaviors, and your speech should reveal love. Even your disciplinary actions should be done with love. Regardless of the appearance of anything that contradicts love, you must choose to love your child.

Yes, it is easy to behave lovingly when one loves. Conversely, one can learn to love from behaving lovingly. You must display loving behavior at <u>all</u> times towards your child, regardless of how you feel.

Agape love is strengthening, powerful, curative, encouraging, and uplifting. When parents exhibit Agape love towards their child, their child will be strengthened, empowered, healed, encouraged, and uplifted.

♥♥♥♥♥♥♥♥

Throughout this chapter, you will be introduced to loving behaviors.

Love your child enough to set guidelines and limits.

Guidelines and limits serve in keeping a child safe and on track. Many parents find it more difficult to impose guidelines and limits as children get older. Establishing the proper guidelines and limits will enable you to enforce them more successfully. Guidelines and limits should have the following elements:

- ☐ age appropriateness
- ☐ can be monitored
- ☐ specific for what you want to accomplish
- ☐ explainable
- ☐ good positive presentation

Real case scenario #4

I never thought I would have to set guidelines and limits for what my children could post on their walls. However, after returning from a vacation, my 16-year-age son decided to hang posters of girls in thongs, bikinis, and very skimpy lingerie in his room.

When I walked into his room, aback I was taken. I thought to myself, "No, no." It took me at least a week to institute my limits. Proper presentation was the key. I recruited his little sister.

As his sister and I walked into the room, I told her to look at the wall. Looking into my son's eyes, I began, "Son, I know you love your little sister. She comes into your room a lot. If she sees those pictures, she will think girls have to dress like that to get attention from boys. After all, they got attention from you."

We had a good conversation, and the pictures were covered up within a day. When his sister and I returned to the room the next day, he had hung a picture of four pretty teenaged girls in a classroom with clothes on and books opened.

As parents, we must explain (not defend) our positions. The difference between explaining and defending is that explaining is done to the level of comprehending why the decision was made. Defending is done when trying to justify the 'rightness' of the decision.

Parents, there are many people who will give your child misunderstanding when you fail to give understanding.

Real case scenario #5

Many students drive to school daily. A student receives a learner's permit at 15 1/2 years of age and a license at age 16. A month later, the student gets a car. One morning, the student is running late for school. The student crashes and dies in a car accident. It is concluded that the student was driving at a high rate of speed. The parents are distraught and filled with guilt.

Why guilt? Generally, guilt comes from knowing what you should do, but failing to do it and realizing that the failure has direct or indirect consequences. If you are feeling guilty about something, STOP. This book has not been written to make one feel guilty.

If you see yourself in this scenario, know that there are many people who stand in prayer with you for a healing. You see, people can express Agape love over many miles for others. For we know, this is truly a tragedy.

Statistic 1:

The Center for Disease Control (CDC) lists automobile accidents as the number one cause of teen deaths. On average, one teen death occurs every 91 minutes.

Factors contributing to teen vehicle crashes include inexperience, low rates of seat belt use, alcohol, and text messaging.

<u>Love your child enough to get involved in their schooling.</u>

Attending school is just one means of educating your child for success. Schools are designed to teach knowledge and skills, develop abilities, disseminate information, and provide certain types of equipment and tools. When one attends school, one is engaging in a formal educational setting. Formal education can be private or public (provided by the government and paid for by taxes).

There are other means of educating, which usually occur outside of school. Enrichment programs, self-education, travel, and private tutors fall under this category. These activities are known to educate in an informal manner and tend to be very costly.

The school's role is to make sure that every member of society achieves a certain level of education. The purpose of education is to ensure that everyone can contribute to and function positively within society.

Whether private or public, education is not free and can be terminated once an individual has shown total disregard for the educational process. Termination of a person's right to an education can be short-term (1 day) or long-term (total expulsion). Either way, suspension from any educational process interrupts a child's academic climb and hinders a child from reaching his/her full potential. Being out of the classroom also causes a child to be deprived of vital knowledge, skills, information, equipment, and materials. In addition, a lengthy absence from school limits a child's ability to perform at an acceptable physical and analytical level. Lastly, being out of the classroom affects a child's positioning, and decreases a child's opportunities.

Education in the United States of America, in most states, is compulsory until a child reaches 16 years of age.

Reader, did you know enough at 16 years of age to become a successful, contributing, functioning adult?

I didn't.

Reader, do you think that at 16 years of age a child will know enough to become a successful, contributing, functioning adult?

Think.

Real case scenario #6

A parent refuses to meet for scheduled parent conferences. The child's behavior and the lack of parental involvement eventually cause the child to be expelled from traditional school.

The child is sent to an alternative school due to behavioral problems. However, the parent still refuses to support the school or attend any parent conferences. The parent blames the alternative school as the cause of the child's behavior.

One day, the child arrives at school sick, and the parent is called. The parent admits to sending the child to school sick and refuses to pick up the child from school. The mother finally comes to school, only after receiving a phone call from the school stating that she needs to see about her child, or else DFACS will be called. The parent does not want to attend a conference. Instead, she asks that her child be transferred to another school. The transfer is denied. The parent then asks school administrators for a ride home.

A week later, the child is suspended for ten days from the behavioral alternative school.

> Parents, how different could this scenario have been if the parent had been actively and positively involved in her child's education?

Here is an indication. Every day, parents and teachers collaborate to hammer out strategies, revise plans, and monitor the performances of children/students. Day after day, children/students are increasing and reaching their full academic potential.

Love your child enough to know your child and know about your child.

In a conversation with my brother, I listened to him discuss the topics that interest his co-workers. He said that he did not understand how men could sit around and discuss everything about an athlete or team. He continued, "Some of these guys can tell you how many points per game a player has, his playing strategy, even the teams he played on years ago." He told me the history of teams his co-workers would discuss and argue. He was truly fascinated about the amount of information his co-workers shared about people who did not know them.

At that point, my brother made a profound statement. He said that some of his co-workers had the audacity not to know much about their children. They would make excuses about not seeing their children and why they were not involved in their children's lives. They would even try to justify the lack of support they provided to their children and the lack of knowledge they had concerning their children. I remember shaking my head in agreement with his comments. I thought about some remarks that I have heard from parents:

*I did not know my child had a reading problem until he was in the 5th grade.

*I never saw my child do homework, so I thought he did not have any.

*My child should not be failing. Those 35 absences were excused. I did not know the work had to be made up.

*Do you know the names of my child's teachers?

*My child told me that he had permission from the

school to leave school early on Fridays.

*A child receives a 'D' for first semester. The parent comes to school after receiving the child's third quarter grade, which is an 'F'. The parent states, "I didn't know my son was having difficulty in this class."

*During the school year, the parent calls and asks, "What time does school start?"

*During the school year, the parent calls and wants to know where the school is located and how to get there.

Parents, who do you know more about?

Parents, do you know more about someone who does not know you or your child?

Think.

♥♥♥♥♥♥♥♥

OK parents, guardians, and caretakers, do not shake your head. Do not be ashamed if you see yourself in some of these examples. Just stop the behavior.

I truly believe that you are reading this book because you want the best for your child. You want your child to reach his/her full potential. You want your child to succeed in school and in life. You are on the right path. You can only change to what you give ear.

In today's world, it is important for our children to get a good education. My mother always told me:

Use your God given common sense and get a good education.

Love your child enough to teach knowledge and understanding.

Why is it important for people to have both?

The next real case scenario reflects one of the consequences caused by a lack of knowledge and understanding.

Real case scenario #7

A day spa lists a want-ad for a Massage Therapist w/license. A man responds to the advertisement and inquires about the "Mes... The...ra...." The spa's human resource person quickly states, "Massage Therapist", realizing the man is having a problem pronouncing the words. The man continues, "I see you ask for a license. I don't have a license, but I have a State I.D."

As you probably already have concluded, real case scenario #7 is what we do not want to happen. However, I know some of you might admit that you know people like this, people who really have a difficult time functioning in society. Somewhere, the education ball was dropped.

Remember, we want our children to be fruitful. Do not drop the ball with your child's education. Do not give up on your child. God has not given up on you.

Love is patience

Have you ever tried to learn and gain an understanding of a concept, and you just were not getting it? Several days later as you are doing an unrelated task, the understanding hits you on the head like a rock as it is revealed. In essence, although you availed yourself to the knowledge, the understanding came later. Children, just like adults, develop their intellect at different times.

Remember, your child is learning about self and the world. In addition, many children are engaged in several tasks, such as school, ballet, swimming, karate, etc. Likewise, they may be affected by your struggles, such as alcoholism, debt, divorce, etc. In spite of everything, children rely on us for engagement, nurturance, and support. When they have problems, their problems must be solved. When they have homework, they must be helped. When they want to talk, they must be heard; someone must listen.

Real case scenario #8

A child is doing homework. The mother comes home from work exhausted. The father enters later after a long day's work. The father sits down to pay bills. The child is having difficulty with fractions and states that she hates homework. The mother comments, "Hate is forbidden. Use that energy to do the work." The brother, who normally helps his sister, is given permission to watch the World Series.

The mother senses that this is a fork in the road for her daughter. The mother makes herself a cup of coffee. The mother and daughter work through the math problems. The daughter's understanding develops around midnight. The daughter is enthusiastic about her accomplishment. Finally, the mother and daughter retire around 12:30 am.

Parents, you must be patient with your child.

Love means enduring

As you may already have figured out, parental involvement in a child's education is a must. Yet, more parents are involved during the early years of their child's education. According to statistics, as a child gets older, the parent becomes less involved.

Which condition requires more parental involvement?

a) From kindergarten through third grade, a child learns to read.

b) After third grade, a child reads to learn.

c) In 6th, 7th, and 8th grades, children are going through hormonal changes, which may affect their self-esteem and self-worth. In addition, their schoolwork may be suffering.

d) In ninth grade, children are separating from many of their friends and going to bigger schools. Plus, children may be experiencing increased peer pressure as they yearn in to fit. Additionally, students have more responsibilities and their teachers and parents have higher expectations of them. Ninth grade is a pivotal point for students.

e) During the eleventh grade, students are struggling with college and career choices. Parents may be trying to get their child to go to a particular college because of tradition, legacy, scholarship, etc. If the child is the first in the family to attend college, there may be an added pressure. SAT and ACT examinations enter the picture. In addition, there is the prom and the whole fear of being rejected.

f) In the twelfth grade, students are struggling with many of the same issues that were discussed in the 11th grade and some added concerns like leaving home. The fear some students have about being away from home is very real.

Now that we have examined some concerns, issues, challenges, and struggles confronting children from K to 12, where is your pull out point?

Parents, when can you not be involved?

Precisely, there is never a time, from K-12, when your child does not need you. Parents, you may be mentally and physically exhausted, but your child needs your loving support and guidance.

Remember: When you run a race, you are more tired at the end than at the beginning.

Love means enduring.

♥♥♥♥♥♥♥

Love rewards the good

'*Job well done,*' is a very positive phrase that everyone loves to hear. It is a rewarding phrase recognizing the good. It is simple and encouraging. It expresses love.

Many phrases, simple gifts, and even a pat on the back serve as a reward to a child who has demonstrated good. Good grades, good behavior, and good manners need to be reinforced with good rewards.

Parents, what do you say, do, or express when your child has done something good?

Think.

One must learn to nurture the *good* in a child. The nurturance must outweigh the attention given when your child does not perform to your expectations.

I was reminded of this when my nine year old child said, "Mom, if we bring home a 'B', we know we have to explain it. And, if we bring home a 'C', oh boy! But, when we bring home all 'A's, you don't say much but "very good'." I asked my children what they wanted. They replied, "More attention for 'A's'.

As I perceived, to them the balance was not there and they needed more nurturance. Therefore, they decided that I should bake their favorite cake when they did the very best they could do.

♥♥♥♥♥♥♥

In the last chapter, I will discuss 'love seeing only good' and 'building from the good'.

45

Parents, choose to love your children.

2

Renewing one's self

Being a parent, guardian, or caretaker is a very demanding role. The responsibilities are numerous, and fulfilling the needs of a child may seem taxing at times. You will get tired. Your tolerance level will be tested. Your child will take you places, emotionally, that you never have been.

The physical and emotional pressures of parenting can cause stressful conditions. Such conditions create wear and tear on the body. Some elevated health risks resulting from stressful conditions are depression, ulcers, headaches, strokes, high blood pressure, anxiety, insomnia, etc.

Discernment is a very powerful weapon in the fight against stress. Take time to learn the stressors in your life. Learn what things, people, and events distress you. Learn how you respond to them. Examine your reaction to stressors. You want your feedback to be calming and to have a positive effect on your body.

Your counterbalance to stressors should aid in managing or reducing overexertion. You do not want your responses to intensify the strain on your body. When necessary, you want to eliminate or avoid unnecessary stressors.

As one of my good friends proclaims,

'If it's not important, it's irrelevant, and what's irrelevant is not important.'

♥♥♥♥♥♥♥♥

When you sign-on to be a parent, you sign-on to be healthy. Your mental, emotional, spiritual, and physical health must be in divine order. For they all work together to rejuvenate, revitalize, and restore the YOU.

As you take care of others, you must take care of self. You must continue to replenish your spirit, mind, and body. Some ways of renewing the YOU are through proper diet, quiet time, rest, relaxation, exercise, and sleep.

Proper diet
What is the proper diet for you? Is it two servings of bread or two servings of fruit? Can you eat fruit and vegetables at the same meal? How much protein do you need? Must you wait thirty minutes after you drink water before you eat?

Individuals have different dietary concerns. Cholesterol, iron, and sugar levels are just a few factors contributing to your nutritional needs. Other components include your mental and physical requirements:

- How many hours do you work?
- Do you exercise?
- What mental work must you perform?
- Are you an educator responsible for teaching students?
- Does your diet support your energy output?

Think.

The answers to these questions will vary from person to person. In other words, in order to know what your body needs as an individual, consult with your doctor. Get a thorough physical examination, and if necessary, have your doctor refer you to a nutritionist for a well-balanced, nutritional diet personalized for you.

Quiet time

Quiet time is when one becomes still. It may be as short as 30 seconds or as long as 30 minutes. Quiet time allows you to renew your spiritual understanding. You may pray during quiet time, talking to GOD. You may meditate during quiet time, listening to GOD. You may praise GOD during quiet time. You may feel the need to ask GOD for guidance and seek God for help. You may want to empty your body temple through confession and profession. Then, allow GOD to fill you up with spiritual guidance and understanding. Sometimes, you may just want to sit and be still.

Quiet time may be used for visualization. Picture how you want your day to unfold. Create in your mind a vision of positive events, which you want to focus on throughout the day.

Keep this image in your mind, and center your thoughts on it.

Conceptualization is a power tool in creating your reality. Your thoughts have energy associated with them. Therefore, negative thoughts put negative energy out into the universe and positive thoughts deposit positive energy into the universe. Keep in mind, *'Like Attracts Like'*. Remember, the Power of the Christ is within you. The Power of the Christ within you will go forth to bring into existence that which you think and speak. Overtime, you will manifest your thoughts into reality.

Quiet time may be used as prevention or an intervention. Before the ordeals of the day begin, sit and think about what may happen during the day. You may need to devise or revise an effective plan for the constant struggles in your life. You can prepare to respond positively to those challenges and not allow them to upset you. Visualize a positive outcome. Many problems that you contemplate have solutions; you just have to find them.

♥♥♥♥♥♥♥

Throughout the course of the day, I take quiet moments. These moments are very strengthening to me, and provide that much needed jolt of calm energy. I refocus my thoughts on the vision I have for my life.

Real case scenario #9

As an administrator, there have been times when I've had to tell someone to STOP and BE CALM. Students and staff would hear these words in a calm, reaffirming voice meaning everything would be fine. I would wait several seconds. During those brief seconds, I would say to self, "Everything is in divine order. GOD, give me strength and wisdom. Thank you GOD." Then, I would proceed.

Powerful words were spoken. Something always happened. Negative activity would stop. I would receive spiritual guidance, and GOD would cover me.

When I started using this practice at home, the same results occurred: negative activity stopped; spiritual guidance entered; and GOD covered me.

Shortly before finishing this book, I made a nice warm cup of brewer's yeast, went outside to sit in the morning sun, and simply reaffirmed:

GOD, I know you have a plan for me.
I am not worried.
Thank you GOD.
Thank you.

There are many books on the power of prayer and meditation. Please browse through these books at your favorite bookstore, and purchase one based on your level of spirituality.

Rest and Relaxation

As earlier stated, being a parent is a demanding role. You will get tired. Therefore, you must rest and relax your body. Find time to rest and relax your body. Take up a hobby. Engage in activities that you find relaxing. At work, you may want to take leisure walks.

I love taking vacations, but I found them to be stressful. I thought vacations were supposed to be relaxing. I heard a man confirm my findings. He talked about vacations being nerve-racking. His solution was to take mini weekend vacations throughout the year. He mentioned that such a practice would help eliminate the stress of preparing for that yearly family event. My family tried his idea, and it worked. Therefore, consider taking mini outings.

Have you ever acted like a tourist in the city where you live?

Try it. You may be very surprised.

♥♥♥♥♥♥♥♥

A parent disclosed to me her remedy for keeping her sanity and becoming emotionally sound. She embraces fifteen minutes of solace in her room before dealing with her second job at home.

Others may find the need to decompress before entering the home, leaving the stresses of the day outside. Make your home a nurturing environment by creating a home atmosphere that caters to the renewing of the spirit.

♥♥♥♥♥♥♥♥

In addition, parents need to develop positive supportive friend-ships and relationships. Listen to positive uplifting music. Speak words of life. You will learn that the first step in rest and relaxation is to change with what and whom you associate.

Psalm 103:5

> *Who satisfieth thy mouth with good thing: so that they youth is renewed like the eagles.*

Exercise

Do you come in the house and nearly collapse? Do you quickly become tired and irritable? Are you barely keeping your eyes open while driving home from work?

If you answered yes, then you are showing signs of a low energy level. You need more energy. Exercise is a way to build your energy reserves. Consult with your doctor to initiate a proper exercise program.

Sleep

Sleep is the most important curative process in the human body. In spite of this, the significance of sleep is benched by diet and exercise. Looking at advertisements, one will notice that those for diet and exercise far outnumber sleep ads.

Too many people are unaware of the healing events taking place during sleep. Shakespeare called sleep "nature's soft nurse," referring to its restorative effects on the body.

During sleep:

- ➢ growth hormones are circulated
- ➢ tissue and organ repairs occur
- ➢ the crucial immune system in regenerated

Statistic 2:

The average person needs eight hours of sleep. If we are regularly deprived of sleep, our energy level, effectiveness, concentration, and consciousness decline. Mental ability is reduced by 25% for every 24 hours without sleep.

Parents, relax your mind and body.

Release your energy through mental and physical work.

Refocus your thoughts on the vision you have for your life.

Renew your spirit, mind, and body.

Relax. Release. Refocus. Renew.

3

Conditioning your home for education

EDUCATION STARTS AT HOME. Parents, guardians, and caretakers, you are responsible for creating an educational environment within your home. You must condition your home for education. Conditioning is *the process of shaping the behavior of a person or thing by repeated exposure to particular stimuli, with which new responses become habitually associated.*

In this chapter, we will look at three 'must dos' when conditioning one's home for education: establishing education as a value, creating and maintaining an educational environment, and reinforcing education to guests and visitors.

Valuing Education

Let us start with a working definition of values. Values are things that possess quality with respect to worth, usefulness, and importance. In essence, values rise to the top in terms of importance and worth. Values warrant some level of protection. Values establish order and priority. Values guide behavior. Values are reinforced day in and day out.

As parents, guardians, and caretakers, you are responsible for instituting values in your households. Some families have values passed down through generations. If this is not the case, then you must establish household values.

Take time out to list ten family values.

Is education on the list?

I hope that it is. If it is not, it should be. Students who value education do better in school. During my tenure as a classroom teacher, I recognized a common factor among students who excelled in school; their families valued education.

♥♥♥♥♥♥♥♥

How would your child respond to the following questions or directives?

- Is education a value in our household?
- How can an education improve the quality of your life?
- Name several ways in which you use education.
- List ten family values and <u>prioritize</u> them.
- Identify ways in which we reinforce education in this household.

The answers to these questions will indicate if you have transferred your value of education to your child. Your values must become a part of your child's value system. Once done, a child begins to desire the value, and protect the value. Then, parents can reinforce the value and when appropriate, issue rewards.

Table 3-1 Educational Attainment vs. Income

Highest Education Level Achieved	Annual Income			
	(2005)	(2004)	(2003)	(2002)
Professional Degree	$113,181	$104,585	$104,596	$103,475
Doctoral Degree	$91,881	$92,413	$84,018	$86,412
Master's Degree	$67,127	$65,423	$61,422	$59,673
Bachelor's Degree	$54,327	$51,296	$50,758	$50,260
Associate Degree	$37,954	$36,309	$35,829	$33,927
Some College	$35,003	$33,919	$33,262	$32,996
High School Diploma	$28,335	$27,426	$26,817	$26,161
High School Non-Graduate	$18,464	$17,503	$17,246	$17,256

Statistic 3:

Table 3-1 Educational Attainment vs. Income Statistics: The CPS (Current Population Survey) is a joint project between the

Department of Labor Statistics and the US Census Bureau. According to the Annual Demographic Survey/March Supplements (produced by the CPS) for people 25 years and older, the Mean Income based on Education Achievement is referenced in Table 3-1.

This information yields a real perspective about the monetary value of education. Discuss this information with your child.

Parents, do not make the mistake of assuming that your values are your child's values.

Never ever, assume.

♥♥♥♥♥♥♥♥

Creating and maintaining an educational environment

What things in your house shout, '*This house values education?*' Do you have...

> dictionaries, encyclopedias, a thesaurus, computer with internet access, printer, educational software (math, science, school curricula, Microsoft office, etc.), current news magazines, informational television (The Discovery Channel, The Learning Channel, CNN, etc.), family bookcase, educational and strategic games, SAT/ACT/ ITBS/Stanford Nine test prep materials, an appropriate place for your child to study, extra school supplies, a copy of your child's schedule on the refrigerator, school contact information on the refrigerator, your child's teachers' contact information on the refrigerator, and the school calendar on the refrigerator?

Go ahead and ask, 'Why on the refrigerator?' Some reasons are listed below:

- This undertaking strengthens the theory that you will stay in contact with your child's teachers.
- If you have teenagers, they need to know that you can get in touch with their teachers at anytime, and that you know the names of their teachers.
- Your child will see that you know what is going on at the school.
- Perception is reality to children. When the child believes that the parents will follow through on communicating with the teachers and the school, these tasks already have been accomplished.

In addition, a bookcase should be in every child's room - providing a place for your child's favorite reading material. This act upholds the importance of reading and the acquisition of knowledge.

♥♥♥♥♥♥♥

Readers, my house speaks *EDUCATION!* Better yet, my house echoes:

> *SUCCESS IS THE ONLY OPTION!*
> *THERE IS NO EXCUSE FOR FAILURE!*
> *THERE IS NO EXCUSE FOR NOT LEARNING!*
> *HELP IS ALWAYS AVAILABLE!*

♥♥♥♥♥♥♥

It is crucial to maintain a learning environment in the home. Background information, familiarity, and expectations are three important factors, which have been identified to impact student participation, performance, and success in the classroom. Vitally important is the need for the home learning environment to reinforce and connect with the school's learning environment. This influential environment increases the child's overall academic achievement in school.

I often say that too many students have been condition in home environments that are widely disconnected from the school's environment. Because of this conditioning process, when some students enter the school building, it's like they are entering a foreign country.

Study Tip for Parents

1. Start reading to your child at a very early age.
2. Create a quiet place for your child to study.
3. Check your child's homework and other assignments, everyday.
4. Monitor the time your child spends watching television, using the computer for recreational activities, and talking on the telephone.
5. Encourage your child to read books, magazines, newspapers, and journals.
6. Meet with your child's teachers before problems arise.
7. Inform your child's school and teachers of changes in the home that may affect your child's ability to stay focused or attend school.
8. Assist your child in securing the materials needed to

complete projects and assignments.

9. Talk to your child, and encourage him/her to do well in school.

10. Make sure your child arrives at school everyday on time and prepared to learn.

Reinforcing educational values to family, guest and visitors

Remember, education is a family affair. Get everyone involved. Extended family members can be very helpful, especially with tutoring, calling schools, searching for learning aids, monitoring and supporting a child, helping with school projects and pro- grams, recognizing weaknesses/deficiencies/strengths, etc.

For the most part, my family appreciates the rewards of a quality education. In spite of this, there exists disparity between the appropriate behaviors that family members believe help chil- dren succeed in school. However, my friends and I use similar strategies. Remember, I can pick my friends, and I choose peo- ple with similar values.

Real case scenario #10

Due to a family member's illness, my son stayed with my sister for a semester. His grades, prior to, and after the stay, were A's and B's. I would call my sister and ask, "How is he doing in school?" My sister would reply, "Fine." As I continued, I would ask her, "Did you check his homework?" She would re- spond, "He said, 'he did it.'"

Sometimes, I felt I already knew the outcome. When my sister received his third quarter grades, she was shocked. There were C's and D's on his report card. When we spoke, she said, "I trusted him." I replied, "It is not about trust. He is a child.

He is programmed to test you. You have to check everything. Once he believes you will check, you only have to keep up the perception."

His grades were improved on the fourth quarter report.

Reader, my sister is a smart, intelligent computer analyst by trade, and like me, she values education. Yet, in this case, one can see how family can differ on how schoolwork should be monitored. My sister believes in trust. My expert advice is, *'When it comes to your child's education, it is better to know'.*

♥♥♥♥♥♥♥♥

Let us continue.

Ok, parents, 'Who is walking through your door?' Look at your family and friends. Which individuals reinforce positive educational values? Which ones do not? Parents, your most precious valuable asset is at stake - your child. You must acknowledge people who are negative, pessimistic, not particularly bright, and of questionable character. If you choose to continue a relationship with these people, set ground rules. For example:

1. Do not allow them to give educational or career advice to your child.
2. Do not leave your child's mind alone with them.
3. Stay in a hotel when you visit them.

Parents, you have limited control over your child's interactions outside the home. Therefore, take the maximum initiative when it comes to environments and situations you can command.

Parents, condition your home for education.

4

Communication...Schooling...Education

Communication to learn your child

Communication is both verbal and non-verbal. Communication is a means of learning your child. From the time your child is a baby to your child's adult stage, you must learn and know about your child.

Parents, I want you to stop and write down everything you know about your child. I know this can be challenging, but you need to be honest.

Real case scenario #11

After her retirement, my mother would read and talk to my son all the time. Due to these interactions, my son learned to read with ease. He grasped concepts very easily. Therefore, in addition to his homework, I would give him extra assignments. Although he quickly completed his work, his work lacked neatness.

Such was not the case with my second child. Things were different. My mother was older, I worked, and with two children, I was exhausted most days. I did not realize the advantage my son had until my daughter began having difficulties reading. My daughter was going to first grade having poor reading skills. I was totally dumbfounded and unprepared for what I needed to do to help her. We were going through a challenge that I knew we had to overcome.

In addition to this challenge, my child was very sensitive. I was struggling, and I really needed to learn my daughter. It was during the summer of 1999 when I learned my daughter. The by-product was I learned a great deal about self.

I thought about many things during that summer. I realized that I never really had to teach basic skills. I was a high school science teacher, mostly of 11th and 12th graders. By the time students entered my class, they already knew how to read. Well, the summer of 1999 was the season of reading.

In teaching my child reading skills, I learned not to raise my voice. Remember, my child was very sensitive, and she would tear-up. Once, during an outing to the library, I lost it. I just yelled, "How come you're not getting this? We keep going over this." Needless to say, she started crying. It later dawned on me that, unconsciously, I was comparing my daughter to her older brother. In that mechanical response, I was putting her down.

I had to step back and learn my daughter. My daughter has great attributes. She is honest, neat, determined, steadfast, analytical, and very perceptive.

In addition, I had to learn me. I had to learn my tolerance level during that time, two hours - maximum. I had to learn pa-

tience. I had to look at my daughter with loving eyes. Moreover, I would pray to GOD for guidance and that my daughter would get it - soon.

It was during this time that I renewed and strengthened my relationship with an educational supply store. Of the many items I purchased, one stands out - a reading skills book with cassette tapes. Whenever I reached my tolerance level, my daughter could continue developing her reading skills on her own, in the privacy of her own room. She probably enjoyed this more than I. I also purchased a wonderful bingo game, which reinforced sight words.

*As a reward and for fun, my daughter and I would visit the local bookstore. She would browse through the aisles and select a book. I became accustomed to purchasing **hot cocoa, cappuccino, two pastries, and a book**. By the end of first grade, my child was reading Harry Potter and Mary Kate and Ashley books. My daughter and I still share outings at that notable bookstore and coffee café. The relaxed atmosphere is priceless.*

My daughter did not verbally communicate her challenges. However, she demonstrated some non-verbal communication, such as frustration in completing homework assignments.

♥♥♥♥♥♥♥

Let me interject at this point; it is crucial that your child learns to read proficiently by the end of third grade. Why? The answer is that most curricula, from kindergarten through third grade, teach children to read. After third grade, children read to learn.

Parents, it really is your fault if your child does not learn to read. You can blame whom you want, but the error is with you.

Students learn at different rates, and teachers have limited time to teach reading skills. In disruptive classes, the amount of time is decreased. With twenty or more students in a class, teachers may not be able to provide individualized instruction.

Later in this chapter, I will educate you on learning styles. Knowing your child's unique learning style will aid you in teaching your child.

♥♥♥♥♥♥♥♥

Parents, <u>you</u> are the backbone and the originator of your child's success. Parents, <u>you</u> determine how much time is spent on homework, if your child will be absent from school, and if your child will have needed materials. Parents, <u>you</u> decide if your child will get extra tutoring, if your child will study for a test, if your child will be on time for school, etc. Parents, if you are weak in your roles, your child will be weak in his/her skills.

Parents, remember that <u>You</u> are the Power behind your Child's Success.

♥♥♥♥♥♥♥♥

Let us continue.

Has your child displayed symptoms of hearing or vision difficulties?

My brother is a classic example of a child who was not properly diagnosed with dyslexia. His teachers wanted to put him in the *'Special Room'*. Today, we call it the special needs program, and many children are benefiting from the extra resources. At that time, it was the *Special Room,* and it did not meet anyone's needs. Students, who were behind in their classes or labeled a discipline problem, were assigned to this room.

My mother, an intelligent woman with loads of common sense, took my brother to a doctor for testing. The test results were normal. However, my brother continued to struggle in school.

After completing elementary school, my brother did not attend traditional schools. Instead, he went to a high school that worked on 'student contractual agreements'. Later, he went to a trade school.

I applaud my mother for taking the time to learn about her son. Even though the schools did not detect my brother's special needs, my mother did not allow the schools to write-off her son. It took years before he was properly diagnosed with dyslexia. Today my brother is a skilled mechanic.

Unfortunately, the traditional way of educating students in America often fails to address unique learning styles. As a result, many children are misplaced in programs. Undiagnosed mental and physical impairments add to this dilemma.

Real case scenario #12

A teacher was called into a conference to meet with the principal, the parent, and the student. The ninth grader's parent was furious, and immediately started 'telling off' the teacher as soon as the principal asked her to state her complaint. The parent loudly stated, "My child received an 'F' for her first quarter grade in this class. I don't know why I wasn't informed. The teacher should have called or sent something home ..."

The principal, looking at the teacher, asked, "Did you follow the school's protocol for issuing progress reports?" The teacher replied, "Yes." The principal asked for documentation.

At this point, the teacher informed the parent that the student had received a progress report every two weeks since the beginning of school. She also provided documentation showing where the student had signed for the reports.

Turning to the child, the parent asked, "Where are the progress reports?" The child answered, "In my book bag." The child retrieved the progress reports and handed them to her parent.

The parent still insisted that the teacher should have called. Finally, the principal asked the parent, "Did you come to Parent Orientation?" The parent said, "No." The principal continued, "This procedure was discussed during orientation and my teacher followed procedure. Therefore, you must commit to improving communication between you and your child. This is a communication problem within the home, not with the school."

Communicating with the teacher and the school

The parent-teacher relationship is very important during a child's early years of education (K-5). From K-5, there are many factors influencing a child's academic success such as socialization with other students, encouragement from teachers, development of unique learning styles, strengthening of skills (i.e. reading, math, analytical, etc.), and the transition from *learning to read* to that of *reading to learn.*

The best way to help your child learn is to know how

your child learns. This requires communicating with the teacher and observing your child's acquisition and demonstration of knowledge.

Learning style and Multiple Intelligence

Learning style refers to the way a child learns. **Multiple Intelligence** is the way in which a child demonstrates learning and intellectual ability. Parents, you are in the best position to help your child succeed in school when you know your child's learning style. Parents, you are in the best position to help your child develop his/her uniqueness when you recognize your child's intellectual ability. Parents, you are in the best position to help your child reach his/her full potential when you know both, your child's learning style and intellectual ability.

Learning styles

For now, I want you to think about how you learn. Do you need to visualize what you are learning? Do you need to see diagrams or pictures? Maybe, you need to talk about things or engage in some other activity in order to learn.

There are three categories of learning styles: **visual learners, auditory learners,** and **tactile/kinesthetic learners**.

1. **Visual learners** learn through seeing, tend to think in pictures, and need material/information presented visually.

   a. **Visual/Verbal learners** - These learners learn best when information is presented visually and in written language format.

   In a classroom, these learners may need

ideas and information reinforced with visuals aids (e.g. overhead transparencies, diagrams), which are explained. These students tend to learn well from videos.

b.　**Visual/Non-verbal learners** – These learners learn best from visual displays, including illustrated textbooks, overhead transparencies, flip-charts, and handouts.

In a classroom, these learners may focus on the teachers' non-verbal communication (body language and facial expressions), and draw pictures or take notes to absorb information.

2.　**Auditory learners** learn through listening. They learn best through verbal exchange, such as lectures, reading text aloud, discussions, conversing with others, talking things through, and listening to what others have to say.

These learners may ask many questions. Elements of speech, such as tone of voice, pitch, and speed, are interpreted by auditory learners for understanding and significance.

3.　**Tactile/kinesthetic learners** learn through doing, moving, and touching. In education, the term used is, the 'hands-on approach'. Basically, these learners like to build it, take it apart, explore it, and do it in order to learn it and understand it.

In a classroom, they may find it hard to sit still for long periods of time because of their need for activity and exploration, and not because they are hyperactive or have a behavioral problem or disorder. These learners are good at creating learning environments that sustain other kids' interests.

Discussion

Parents, you should begin to comprehend the worth in knowing your child's learning style. This information tends to trigger all types of responses from '*that's why*' to '*the teacher needs to...*'

Let us slow down for a moment. Remember there are 19 to 34 other students in your child's classroom, all with different learning styles. The teacher has to incorporate a diverse range of teaching and learning methodologies during class to help <u>all</u> children. Therefore, a child who learns best by doing needs to be inactive for a period of time, so as not to distract children who need verbal explanation. In addition, students with dyslexia have a wide range of learning styles.

The value of knowing your child's learning style is in the relationship with the class setting. For example, a visual learner may need to sit towards the front. I have observed teachers assist parents, of kinesthetic learners, in teaching strategies at home that will help the child sit still for 15-20 minutes.

In elementary school, it is very important to eliminate a child's frustrations quickly, especially those frustrations surrounding difficulties in learning. If ignored, frustrated students may quickly feel defeated in the education process and 'shut down'.

During my teaching career, two of my colleagues and I taught the same course. One of my colleagues used more of a hands-on/verbal/visual teaching style, the other used more of a visual/verbal/hands-on teaching approach, and I used more of a verbal/visual/hands-on teaching method. One of my students confronted me about struggling in my class. I asked a few key questions and determined that she needed more visual aids, more than what I used. I spoke with my colleague who used more of a visual/verbal/hands-on teaching design. The student was transferred into my colleague's class and experienced greater success. On the other hand, many college bound, pre-med students enrolled in my class.

Differentiated Instruction/Learning

Differentiated instruction is an approach to teaching essential content in ways that address the varied learning needs of students with the goal of maximizing the possibilities of each learner. Examples of differentiated instruction and learning techniques are CDs, books, lectures, videos, projects, and portfolios.

Multiple Intelligences

Conceived by Howard Gardner, Multiple Intelligences are eight different ways to demonstrate intellectual ability (proficiency, aptitude, cognitive understanding, etc.). Gardner rationalized that intelligence based on I.Q. testing is too limited. Multiple Intelligence accounts for an expanded range of human potential in people. Examine the multiple intelligences' list:

1. **Spatial Intelligence (space smart)** – ability to utilize space in essence, the ability to position one's self in large -scale and small intimate spatial environments
2. **Linguistic Intelligence (word smart)** – ability to use words and language

3. **Logical/Mathematical Intelligence (number/reasoning smart)** – ability to use reason, logic, and numbers
4. **Bodily/Kinesthetic Intelligence (body/athletic smart)** – ability to control body and movements and handle objects skillfully
5. **Musical/Rhythmic Intelligence (music smart)** – ability to produce music and detect the elements of music such as sounds, rhythms, and patterns
6. **Interpersonal Intelligence (people smart)** – ability to relate and understand others; empathizers
7. **Intrapersonal Intelligence (self-smart)** – ability to self-reflect and be aware of one's inner state of being
8. **Naturalist Intelligence (Nature smart)** – ability to recognize and categorize plants, animals, and other objects

The multiple intelligences' list is a working list. Other intelligences include **Existential and Spiritual Intelligences.**

Discussion

Here again, the value of knowing about multiple intelligence is in the relationship with the instructional setting. Educational programs that utilize creative arts, music, community service, nature, and volunteer efforts cater more effectively to the diverse intelligences (intellectual abilities) of students.

Parents, you can take advantage of this information by enrolling your child in various enrichment programs. Such programs will help to nurture and develop your child's individual uniqueness. Moreover, they will help your child reach his/her full potential.

Overall

Learning styles and multiple intelligences do not exist in exclusivity. A child does not possess one learning style or one intelligence. A child tends to be more preferential to some than others, consequentially creating a child's unique and distinct learning style.

In addition, do not expect schools to be similar in the types of instructional curricula adopted. Disparities may exist for a variety of reasons, including parents' willingness to pay out -of-pocket expenses for enrichment programs. A shortage of funds may exist due to schools having to replenish textbook supplies because kids destroy them, and the parents refuse to reimburse schools for the costs. Textbooks and vandalism tend to consume more of the school's budget than any other item.

Whether you are the parent of a regular student or special needs child, the foundation for success is knowing your child's learning style(s) and intelligence(s). If your child is musically inclined and the school does not use music in its curriculum, you may want to enroll your child in a music program. Speech and drama guilds will help the verbally challenged child.

❤❤❤❤❤❤❤

Let us continue.

Standardized tests

Standardized tests provide a means of assessing a school or student's performance. Two types of standardized tests often used are criterion reference and norm reference tests. A criterion reference test (CRT), in general, assesses specific goals, purposes, and values considered important to the school such as: school's performance, student's performance of specific tasks, or student's possession of specific knowledge. A norm reference test, such as the Iowa Test of Basic Skills, Stanford Nine, SAT, and ACT, assesses the performance of test takers relative to one another. The basic difference between the two tests is that the criterion-referenced test does not show how your child ranks with his/her peers, and a norm-referenced test does.

Discussion

The biggest mistake parents make is assuming that all standardized tests assess their child's achievement from one year to the next. However, in order to know how far a student has come, one needs to know from where the student started. Parents, learning your child, reviewing and scrutinizing your child's work, and analyzing information received from your child's teachers will help you to measure your child's yearly achievement.

Parents, whenever your child takes a criterion-reference test, you need to know what is being assessed. For example, a CRT designed to evaluate a school's performance will not be valid for assessing the level at which your child can perform, although meeting the criteria is based on overall student performance. Any one of several possible reasons can cause the invalidity:

- the minimum score a student needs to meet a school's performance criteria can be very low, sometimes as low as sixty percent of the total score
- a small amount of knowledge or skill performance relative to the total curriculum is assessed

- the test may be deficient in evaluating '**high order thinking**' skills

Parents, when you examine your child's norm-reference test scores, you will see how many items your child attempted to answer, how many items your child answered correctly, and how your child's scores compare to other students' scores in your child's defined group. Norm-reference test scores provide much useful information by detailing the level at which your child functions in many different skill areas. Parents, if you want to know how your child's school compares to other schools, analyze the school's average <u>norm reference test scores</u>.

♥♥♥♥♥♥♥♥

Note: In a classroom, educational activities can be divided into three areas or domains. They are the cognitive, affective, and psychomotor educational domains.

1. **Cognitive educational domain** - involves knowledge and intellectual skills.
2. **Affective educational domain** - involves dealing with emotions (values, motivation, appreciation, etc.).
3. **Psychomotor educational domain** - involves physical movement, motor skills, and coordination.

♥♥♥♥♥♥♥♥

Let us continue.

Many parents wonder how their 'A' student can score low on standardize tests. The answer generally falls between two areas: poor testing skills and poor academic (hence; cognitive) skills. There are many comprehensive books on enhancing test-taking skills (timing, eliminating answers, tips, etc.) that can be purchased at your local bookstore. I will focus on the more complex issue of cognitive skills. Is your child learning, how much does your child knows, standardized testing, and grades are all topics that revolve around cognitive education.

Bloom's Taxonomy
Bloom's taxonomy categorizes six levels of cognitive domains from simple recall (knowledge level) to making choices based on reasonable argument (evaluation level). Refer to Figure 4-1.

Fig. 4-1

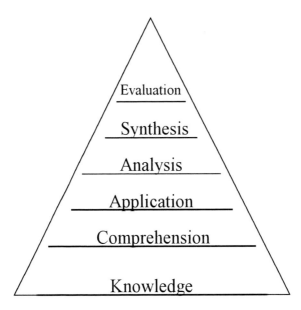

Referencing the pyramid, knowledge is the most basic cognitive ability, and evaluation is the highest cognitive aptitude.

Table 4-1:

Cognitive Levels	Skill	Some Key Words
Knowledge	Recall data	Define, match, list, name, recall, recognize, select
Comprehension	Understanding data	Explain, express, describe, discuss, restate
Application	Using data Knowing when to use data.	Interpret, apply, employ, demonstrate
Analysis	Seeing patterns in data. Applying data to new situations.	Analyze, compare, contrast, criticize, calculate, differentiate
Synthesis	Draw conclusion. Build/construct from diverse elements.	Construct, compose, formulate, invent, integrate
Evaluation	Support argument. Discriminate between ideas and information.	Assess, support, discriminate, judge, critique, defend

Table 4-1 shows the cognitive aptitude with its respective skill ability/abilities. In addition, you will notice key words that give guidance as to which cognitive level is being addressed.

Parents, take a moment to familiarize yourselves with Figure 4-1 and Table 4-1.

♥♥♥♥♥♥♥

Parents, teachers can assess learning based on different levels of cognitive ability for students at any age, using age appropriate methods.

Here is the answer to the question, *'How can my 'A' student score low on standardized tests?'* Many teachers spend as much as 70% of their instructional time teaching knowledge and comprehension skills. Most standardized test questions, however, require students to use 'Higher Order Thinking' skills: application, analysis, and synthesis.

Summing it up, when teachers focus most of their instruction at the knowledge and comprehension levels, a student can have a *'B to A'* average and be ill-equipped to do well on a standardized test.

Discussion

Bloom's taxonomy is a great way to monitor the cognitive development of your child by examining his/her work. Simply make a grid, log assignments, and check which cognitive levels are addressed. Take a look at the **Assignment Evaluation Sheet** on page 86. An example **Assignment Evaluation Sheet** is on page 87.

ASSIGNMENT EVALUATION SHEET

ASSIGNMENT CHARACTERISTICS				ASSIGNMENT SKILL LEVEL (BLOOM'S TAXONOMY)					
Title	Independent	Group	Grade	Knowledge	Comprehension	Application	Analysis	Synthesis	Evaluation

In the following example **Assignment Evaluation Sheet**, notice the student's low performance on independent assignments.

EXAMPLE ASSIGNMENT EVALUATION SHEET

| ASSIGNMENT CHARACTERISTICS | | | | ASSIGNMENT SKILL LEVEL (BLOOM'S TAXONOMY) | | | | | |
Title	Independent	Group	Grade	Knowledge	Comprehension	Application	Analysis	Synthesis	Evaluation
Sponge 1	X		18/20	X	X				
Pangaea		X	95/100	X	X	X	X		
Sponge 2	X		10/20	X	X	X			
Cells/Labeling		X	93/100	X	X	X	X		
CRL Cells		X	100/100	X	X	X	X	X	X
Chapter 3		X	99/100	X	X	X	X		
CBL Photosynthesis		X	100/100	X	X	X	X	X	X
Chapter 1	X		86/100	X	X	X	X	X	X
Chapter 18	X		72/100	X	X	X	X	X	X
Chapter 2	X		75/100	X	X	X			
Notebook	X		86/100	X					
Tissues Paper	X		83/100	X	X	X			
Lab-Plants		X	95/100	X	X	X	X		
Test	X		76/100	X	X	X	X	X	X

Parents, you want your child's teachers to provide high quality teaching, learning, evaluation, and assessment.

Hint #1

You may consider leaving your child in a class that is strict and more challenging if the teacher is loving, nurturing, fair, and respectful.

Here is a list of questions you want to ask your child's teachers.

1. How do you communicate with parents?
2. What skills are lacking in my child?
3. What skills does my child need to improve?
4. What unique talents have you noticed in my child?
5. What suggestions can you give me on how to help my child improve?
6. What teaching, assessment, and evaluation methodologies do you overwhelmingly use?
7. Are there any supplementary materials (software, homework guides, etc.) that you recommend I purchase and use?
8. How often do you send progress reports?

Parents, a high quality education starts with high expectations and high standards. Parents, it is your responsibility to set expectations and standards for your child. Parents, you must work with your child's teachers to keep high standards and high expectations in the classroom; you must help keep your child's teachers honest about teaching.

Parents, low expectations and low standards contribute to classroom management problems. Therefore, it is no surprise that unruly classrooms and frequent disciplinary incidences are signs of low expectations and low standards. This same philosophy is applicable to a school's environment. Low standards and low expectations contribute to increased disciplinary problems in a school.

A positive working relationship between the parent and teacher is a very valuable asset in identifying your child's needs and helping your child succeed in school. A child whose parents are involved in his/her education will excel in school.

Parents, you have been given what you need to help your child learn. You have the knowledge. Now, it is time to make the choice. Choose to help your child succeed in school.

Parents, <u>you</u> are the Power behind your Child's Success.

♥♥♥♥♥♥♥

<u>Communication to prevent and resolve issues</u>
You and your child have responsibilities in maintaining a safe, quality learning environment in school and in the classroom. It is very important that communication in the home and with the school reinforce a safe, quality learning environment. Therefore, the following communication is imperative:

89

❖ Discuss the school's disciplinary code with your child.

❖ Prevent problems by having your child follow school and classroom policies.

❖ Meet your child's teachers within the first 2-3 weeks of school.

❖ Give correct contact information to the school and to the teachers.

❖ Visit the school to observe your child.

❖ Volunteer one hour per month in your child's school.

❖ Recruit family members to help with your child's schooling and education.

❖ Document! Document! Document!
Document every time you call the school, with whom you spoke, the reason for the call, and the results.

❖ Immediately conference with the teacher and/or principal to resolve any concerns about teacher competency or the classroom environment.

❖ Do not teach your child bad habits and expect your child to be an angel in school and in the classroom. Remember, your child will mimic your behavior; your child will expose your conduct.

Real case scenario #13

A middle grade student brought a CD player into the classroom. The teacher caught the student listening to the CD player and confiscated it. The teacher informed the student that it would be returned to him when more consistent and appropriate behavior was demonstrated.

Several months passed, and the student wanted his CD

player. The teacher refused, and the student started cursing at the teacher and making threatening comments. Consequently, the teacher referred the student to the assistant principal.

The assistant principal removed the student from class and took the student to an office. The assistant principal also tried to get the student to calm down. However, the student continued ranting, raving, cursing, and threatening the teacher.

At this point, the assistant principal retrieved the child's file and attempted to contact the parents. He made several attempts to contact a parent, guardian, or friend of the child, but all available numbers were disconnected. The assistant principal asked the student for a contact number, but did not get one.

The student stormed out of the office and continued the belligerent behavior. Finally, the principal was called and informed of the situation. The principal was successful in getting the student into an empty room, and a counselor was summoned. The counselor tried to calm the student.

Fifteen minutes later, the student burst out of the room and shouted, "I will blow this school up." Because of this comment, the student was arrested and convicted on charges of making terrorist threats in a public school.

The district sent the student to a behavioral alternative school for the remainder of the school year. In addition, the judge sentenced the student to two years probation and eighty hours of community service.

I have known parents to give incorrect contact information, intentionally, or outright refuse to give contact information. The reasoning they claim is, '*they are tired of the child and being contacted by the school.*'

Let us continue.

Parents, you must instruct your child on procedures to follow for resolving conflict and dealing with peer pressure. Also, instruct your child on procedures for teacher and school initiated concerns. In my family, we have instructed our children to do the following:

A) Inform the teacher if you are experiencing problems with another student. If the problem involves a student verbally assaulting, threatening, or bullying you, contact a parent. When necessary, we will be there within fifteen minutes. If the problem involves a physical assault, use common sense, strategize, and defend yourself. Never leave the school if you feel you will be harmed. Notify the principal and stay in the office. (Note: Never presume that you know how a person/ bully will act.)

B) Concerns about a teacher need to be discussed with a parent. Once home, immediately inform us, your parents, of the issue. We will work out the best course of action to resolve any student-teacher differences. (Note: The process could range from student-teacher conference to student-parent-teacher conference to parent-teacher-administrator conference and anything in between.)

C) Always blame and use parents as your way out when experiencing peer pressure. Some excuses: I have to go and call my mom or dad; my mom will kill me; or

I have to go meet my dad.

D) Always inform us (your parents) of possible school or classroom infractions on your part.

E) School concerns initiated by the teacher or the school will also be given top priority. If called by the teacher or school, when necessary, we will be there within fifteen minutes.

In my home, we have discussed and role-played different scenarios.

Example: **Bullying**

Dialogue about bullying resulted in the development of a *talk and walk* procedure, which is to position yourself in the presence of an administrator or other helpful adult. Never leave school if there is the slightest chance of being harmed. Contact us. Once you have the opportunity, immediately document everything that occurred and led to the bullying, including the bullying itself.

Discussion

Documentation is very vital in any school related issue, especially bullying. Parents, you want to start a paper trail and notify school administrators. If nothing is done, get a lawyer and take legal action. Bullying that results in physical or emotional harm may require that you file criminal and/or civil charges against the perpetrator and his/her guardians. Again, consult with an attorney. (Note: Immediately request a transfer if your child's safety is jeopardized.)

Parents, you want your child to be in a safe, quality learning environment.

♥♥♥♥♥♥♥♥

Positive strategies for resolving conflict can range from changing seats to changing schools. I have known parents to teach their child Chess in order to develop their child's ability to see the big picture (all possible scenarios) and skill to reposition one's self to stop conflict completely. I have also known parents to enroll their child in self-defense classes to teach their child how to defend one's self during a physical assault.

Conversely, I have seen the outcome of parental instructions that have resulted in severe harm and even death to their child. From my experience, the worst conflict resolution commandment is to advise a child to provoke a fight.

Real case scenario #14

A student jumped another female student in the school's stairway because she believed the female student intentionally bumped her in passing. The student who provoked the fight declared, "I was told to fight if someone started something with me."

The mother arrived at the school and said that her words were taken out of context. Even so, the parent of the victim decided to press criminal charges. The student was charged with Battery and could serve jail time if convicted.

Parents, communicate with your child, your child's teachers, and the school. Communication prevents, intervenes, and resolves.

PART II

PARENTS, IT IS YOUR RESPONSIBILITY TO SUPPLY YOUR CHILD'S NEEDS

(FOOD-CLOTHING-SHELTER-HEALTH CARE-LOVE-ENCOURAGEMENT-A SAFE ENVIRONMENT-A SENSE OF BELONGING)

5

Be nurturing; stop neglectful behavior

Over the past 15 years, I have witnessed a sharp increase in the number of students who are neglected. I believe that one of the greatest threats to a safe, quality learning environment is the increasing number of problems and challenges resulting from children being neglected. Because of neglect, every year, there is an increase in the number of students who are sent to school ill, in poor health, and malnourished. Often, these children are emotionally deprived and underdeveloped. Statistics regarding this problem are growing rapidly as society continues to struggle with this tragedy.

The effects of neglect are evident:

- an increase in the number of students who are scared, rude, disrespectful, and violent
- lack of resources to resolve problems and challenges ef-

fectively
- increased number of disruptive classrooms and potentially unsafe schools

♥♥♥♥♥♥♥♥

Throughout my tenure as an educator, I have noticed how frustration and fatigue contribute to parental neglect. I have seen families purchase unaffordable wants, which resulted in overextended households and led to neglectful actions. However, after listening to many parents, I have concluded that most of the excuses for neglectful behavior arise from wrong choices and misplaced values.

In contrast, involved parents possess their own unique characteristics. They tend to sacrifice material items in exchange for having the time to nurture, support, encourage, and share with their children. Involved parents create schedules and support systems for involvement. These parents can get to the school at the drop of a dime.

Parents, it is time to make <u>good</u> choices.

♥♥♥♥♥♥♥♥

Frustration, fatigue, and neglect
Parents, guardians, and caretakers love your children. Provide them with the help and support they need. I make these same suggestions to parents of children who have social challenges (children who may be suicidal, violent, steal, rape, etc.). Do not neglect your children. Be honest about your children.

> **Parents, only when you are honest about your child will you be in the best position to help your child.**

Real case scenario #15

A student, from a private school, entered my class during his senior year. One day, the student came to class smelling like alcohol, and I reported him to the counselor. The counselor confirmed that the student was intoxicated and contacted the parent.

During his stay in my class, the student submitted work after the deadline for the sake of receiving any credit. Once, I caught the student cheating on an exam. When I tried to communicate with the student, he was very arrogant and unresponsive.

The parents never responded to any progress reports and based on information from the counselor, they were not involved in the child's schooling. The student failed to pass the class, and as a result, he was scheduled for a senior retest (second opportunity to take the final). The student failed the retest, and therefore, failed the class.

After receiving his son's grades, the father wanted a conference. The father, the assistant principal, and I met for a conference. The first statement the father made was, "I know my son is an asshole. He's been kicked out of three private schools. I'm just trying to get him in college." At that point, I felt we could talk. We developed a plan and worked together on it. The child passed with a 'D', although the father was hoping for a 'C'.

I believe this father was a caring parent. Even with this belief, I recognized that the father neglected the child based on the following facts:

- During the conference, the father said that he thought the work would not be a problem for the son; the father did not monitor his son's work.
- The father failed to communicate with the teacher and the school about extenuating circumstances affecting the child's academic success.
- The father failed to communicate with the teacher in a timely manner. In effect, he hindered the development and implementation of an effective strategy, which would have helped his son to earn a grade higher than a 'D'.

Based on the comments and actions of the father, I concluded that frustration and fatigue helped form the father's neglectful actions.

Parents, how many times have you been so tired, overburdened, or frustrated to the point where you neglected your child's needs?

Think.

Parents, get more rest, ask for help, and pray. Whatever it takes, <u>do not</u> neglect your child.

♥♥♥♥♥♥♥

Your child engages in an activity that you warned against. Your child's action imposes its own punishment and consequences, but you do not know it. Your child is scared. You are so mad that you tell your child not to talk to you. You never invite your child to discuss the matter. You have distanced yourself from your child. Parents, you have taken the high and mighty road. Parents, you have shut out your child. Parents, your child is suffering, and you are unaware of it.

Real case scenario #16

After lecturing on Sexually Transmitted diseases, a student approached me. The student asked many specific questions about symptoms and effects. The student said, "I've been having a discharge. It's green and smelly." I asked, "How come you didn't go to your parents?" She said, "My mom is mad at me. She found out that I've been having sex."

I immediately walked her to the school nurse and contacted her mother. The mother was furious. Then the student said, "I've had the discharge for several weeks."

Parents, anger and frustration are not reasons to abandon communication with your child.
Your child's medical needs are
your responsibility.
Talk, do not neglect.

Statistic 4:

According to Kaiser Family Foundation, in the U.S., approximately one in four sexually active teens contracts an STD every year. An estimated half of all new HIV infections occur in people under age 25. Most young people are infected through sex.

Overextended households, incorrect choices, and neglect

A common form of neglect occurs when parents are overextended (living above their means).

One of my colleagues has a saying:

If your parents are working full and part-time jobs to pay for the house, SUV, and Mercedes, you are not middle class; you are overextended.

The '*keep up with the Jones*' and '*instant gratification*' mentalities have fashioned another cause of neglect - overextended households. Many parents are in debt, stressed, or absent from home due to working long hours to pay for wants.

Parents, let us try a little exercise. I want you to create three lists (survival list, needs list, and wants list) that clock your work hours based on your hourly income. The lists I have created are based on an average household income of $62,400/yr or $30.00/hr.

List #1: Survival list - List your survival needs (food, housing, basic clothing, household bills, etc.) and how many hours you need to work each week to meet each need.

Example:

- House $190,000 @7%, 30yrs = $1265/mo.   11 hrs/wk
- Food $400/mo   3 hrs/wk
- Car $15,000 @ 6%, 5yrs = $300/mo.   3 hrs /wk
- House insurance & taxes $215/mo   2 hrs/wk
- Household bills $400/mo   3 hrs/wk

- Car Insurance $150/mo   2 hrs/wk
- Family Med. Ins. $400/mo   3 hrs/wk
- Personal & Clothing $250/mo.   2 hrs/wk

List #2: Needs list - List your needs.

Example:

- Car Expense/Other transportation $200/mo   2 hrs/wk
- Schooling/Education $100/mo   1 hr/wk
- State & Federal Taxes $420/mo   4 hr/wk

Analyze both lists.

Analysis:

Lists 1 and 2 total 36 hours per week. However, there is no listing for credit cards, dry cleaning, school uniforms, day care, child enrichment activities or college fund. Likewise, spending time with children is also a need; you must fulfill the child's need for nurturance.

List #3: Wants list - List your wants.
Example:

- Instead of the $15,000 car, you want the $35,000 luxury or a second car

Note: Car adds +$20,000 @ 6%, 5 yrs. or $376 /mo. plus 150/mo car insurance, additional work   + 4 hrs./wk.

Now analyze the lists.

Analysis:

- ✓ Lists 1, 2, and 3 total 40 hours per week.
- ✓ Anyone of the following: credit cards, dry cleaning, life

ins., contributions, entertainment, day care, or college fund will put you over 40 hours per week. You now have to work over-time or a part-time job.
✓ You have created the optimum condition for neglect; you are overextended.

♥♥♥♥♥♥♥♥

Recently, I spoke with a group of students discussing violence in America. They indicated that they could not get around it, and fights occur in every school. Without intention, the group of three students increased to seven. The students were disclosing their perceptions of society.

Let me tell you how the conversation began. I overheard some students discussing fighting. One student was talking about what he would have to do if a particular student decided to fight him. This was a golden moment. It was my cue to intervene, and I did.

Austin: What do you think the other person will do? Better yet, can I give an example?
Student: Yes.
Austin: If you were teasing another student, what do you think the other student would do?
(Several answers were given in this order: 1. get mad; 2. fight me; 3.tease me; 4. hurt me; and 5. kill me. I commented on how interesting that the worst scenario was given last.)
Austin: Suppose he kills you first? (Students shrugged their shoulders). You can't control a person's reaction. That student may just decide to kill you. Most students think a person will react the same way they would, and that's not always the case.

You can't control people nor can you actualize how they will respond.

Student: Yes, I understand, but violence is everywhere. You have to defend yourself.

Austin: Ok. Let's say violence is everywhere – for the moment. Let's say you live to be at least 75 years of age. You graduate at 18 years of age. You are left with 57 years to do things your way, and the chances are slim that you will ever see any of these students again. From my own personal experience, out of a high school graduating class of four hundred students, I've only associated with four students since high school. Trust me; you're not going to see most of these students ever again.

Student: Well, we do try to avoid fights. I mostly fight for family, and family is important.

Austin: True. Family is important.

(At this point, I drew a diagram with two sides and a barrier in between.)

Here's where you are.

(I pointed to the side of the diagram I had labeled high school.)

This is where you will be after high school.

(Pointing to the other side. I had labeled the following terms on this side: college, job, profession, career, and family.).

You have to see beyond high school, and determine how what you do over here (pointing to side 1) will affect you over here (pointing towards side 2).

(I continued pointing, with this back and forth action, while discussing how you must determine what you need to do over here to help you get over there. I could see it in their eyes. They were thinking.)

Austin Cont.: The chances are greater that you will never see these kids again. Don't make choices that could wreck the next 57 years.

Student: What do you want me to do? Walk away?

Austin: If necessary, move or go to another school.

Student: Then, they'll call you a punk, and this is a good school. A lot of rich students go here.

Austin: Yes, they may call you a punk. However, the chances are greater that you will never see them again, and there are more overextended students than rich students.

Students: Yes. You're right.

Austin: Do you believe that just as violence can occur anywhere, good can occur anywhere?

(A short pause occurred.)

Students: Yes.

Austin: How many of you travel and are exposed to the good in society?

Student: Man, my parents work all the time.

Austin: Well, I really want you to find preventable solutions like choosing your friends more wisely, stop butting into other folks business, learn to keep your mouth shut sometimes, focus on getting to the other side – over the barrier, and stop criticizing and putting people down. If you do these things, I guarantee you will get into fewer confrontations. (At that point, one of the students sat straight up.) Plus, expose yourself to the good in society. Travel, meet new people, and try new things.

Your words and actions are powerful. You can build empires, manifest dreams, and create friends with your words, or you can tear people down and start wars. The choice is yours.

The world is yours.

Statistic 5:
According to the Center for Disease Control, homicide is the second cause of death for young people 15-to-24 years of age and the fifth cause of death for young people 10-to-14 years of age.

Discussion
I prayed that I had prevented a confrontation by engaging in this dialogue with the students. Still, this conversation should have been between the students and their parents, guardians, or care-takers.

Parents, you must **share** with your child. Sharing means spending time with your child, talking to your child, and listening to your child. Another very nurturing action is to **touch** your child. Trust me; a daily hug is a wealth of preventative medicine. Every day I hug my children. When I first started this practice, my son was a little apprehensive, but I kept doing it. A *daily hug*, an *I love you*, and a *have a good day* are all apart of their daily nourishment.

Parents, never assume that your child is not being neglected.

♥♥♥♥♥♥♥

Real case scenario #17
A student comments that she did not complete her homework. The student mentions that she had to baby-sit her little brother because her mother went to a "one day sale" at a local store.

*The teacher then asks, "What time did your mother get home."
The student replies, "Around nine-thirty."*

This situation reminds us that we need to eliminate behavior that interferes with meeting a child's need for nurturance.

Teen suicide and neglect

Statistic 6:
According to the Center for Disease Control (CDC), suicide is the third leading cause of death for young people 10-to-24 years of age, surpassed only by car accidents and homicide.

Teen suicide continues to increase. Many professionals, who work with teens, believe this is due to teens spending more time alone and having greater access to lethal weapons. *'They're just being a teenager'*, *'it's a teen thing'*, and *'you know teenagers'* are some beliefs parents accept, which allow them to neglect their children. There is never a moment when your child does not need you. Parents, do not neglect or ignore your child's behavior.

Love, support, care, concern, and communication are important behaviors in your arsenal to prevent suicide. Depression, confusion, new school, new city, instability, anxiety, use of alcohol and drugs, fear of life, sexual identity issues, violent tendencies, divorce, feelings of inadequacy, worthlessness and unwantedness, and physical and sexual abuse are just some of the events that put kids at an increased risk for suicide.

The American Academy of Child and Adolescent Psychiatry gives the following warning signs of adolescents who may try to kill themselves:

- change in eating and sleeping habits
- withdrawal from friends, family, and regular activities
- violent actions, rebellious behavior, or running away
- drug and alcohol use
- unusual neglect of personal appearance
- marked personality change
- persistent boredom, difficulty concentrating, or a decline in the quality of school work
- frequent complaints about physical symptoms, often related to emotions, such as stomachaches, headaches, fatigue, etc.
- loss of interest in pleasurable activities
- not tolerating praise or rewards
- complain of being a bad person or feeling "rotten inside"
- give verbal hints with statements such as "I won't be a problem for you much longer;" "Nothing matters;" "It's no use;" and "I won't see you again."
- put affairs in order, give away favorite possessions, clean room, throw away important belongings, etc.
- become suddenly cheerful after a period of depression
- have signs of psychosis (hallucinations or bizarre thoughts)

In addition to expressing love, care, concern, support, and communication, there are a number of other things parents can do to help their child during difficult times:

- Do not trivialize what your child is going through.
- Do not neglect or ignore your child's behavior.

- Make sure your child has a trusting individual in whom to confide.
- Be positive and reinforce to your child that with help *this too we shall overcome.*
- Get immediate help.

Parents and suicide

I have added this section because parents, for various reasons, are committing suicide more frequently.

Whether you are a parent or child, at the time one is thinking about committing suicide, the thought pattern is that of **'white or black, no gray area.'** In others words, one cannot see a way out. It is a tunnel vision of the worst kind. One cannot see over the hill, across the street, or around the corner. The person is thinking that there is no way out, it will not get any better, and it is unbearable.

It is an emotional bondage for everyone when a loved one is in such a state that renders one to kill one's self. When the person is an adult, and even more a parent, guardian, or caretaker, it can be hard to understand why some life lessons were not learned, experienced, or believed. Life lessons such as:

- ❖ This too shall pass.
- ❖ If you just hold on, joy will come in the morning.
- ❖ All things work out for those who love the Lord.
- ❖ We shall overcome.
- ❖ Trust in the Lord, with all thy understanding.
- ❖ Cast your burdens upon the Lord.
- ❖ The latter will be better than the past.

❖ The 23rd Psalm

> *The Lord is my shepherd; I shall not want.*
>
> *He maketh me to lie down in green pastures; he leadeth me beside the still waters.*
>
> *He restoreth my soul; he leadeth me in the paths of righteousness for his name's sake.*
>
> *Yea, though I walk through the valley of the shadow of death, I will fear no evil; for thou art with me;*
>
> *Thou preparest a table before me in the presence of mine enemies; thou anointed my head with oil; my cup runneth over.*
>
> *Surely goodness and mercy shall follow me all the days of my life; and I will dwell in the house of the Lord for ever.*

Many of our parents and grandparents taught us life lessons that helped us to trust in the Lord when we had little faith, and could not see tomorrow; it was Black and White. They held on until they saw *Gray*. We must hold on until we see *Gray*. We must help our children to see *Gray*.

♥♥♥♥♥♥♥

If you need love, remember that you are always loved:

Romans 8:39

> *Nor height, nor depth, nor any other creature, shall be able to separate us from the **love** of God, which is in Christ **Jesus** our Lord.*

113

1 Corinthians 16:24

> *My **love** be with you all in Christ **Jesus**. Amen.*

2 Corinthians 13:14

> *The grace of the Lord **Jesus** Christ, and the **love** of God, and the communion of the Holy Ghost, be with you all. Amen*

2 Thessalonians 2:16-17

> *Now our Lord **Jesus** Christ himself, and God, even our Father, which hath **loved** us, and hath given us everlasting consolation and good hope through grace,*
>
> > *Comfort your hearts, and stablish you in every good word and work.*

♥♥♥♥♥♥♥♥

If it is forgiveness you need, you got it:

Luke 23: 34

> *Then Jesus said, Father, forgive them for they know not what they do.*

Mark 2: 10-11

> *But that ye may know that the Son of man hath power on earth to forgive sins (he saith to the sick of the palsy).*
>
> > *I say unto thee, Arise, and take up thy bed and go thy way into thine house.*

♥♥♥♥♥♥♥♥

If you have unbearable sorrow, burdens, or pain, give it to GOD:

Psalm 55: 22

> *Cast thy burden upon the LORD, and he shall sustain thee: he shall never suffer the righteous to be moved.*

1Peter 5: 6-7

> *Humble yourselves therefore under the mighty hand of GOD, that he may exalt you in due time.*
> *CASTING ALL YOUR CARE UPON HIM, FOR HE CARETH FOR YOU.*

Psalms 37: 5

> *Commit thy way unto the LORD; trust also in him; And he shall bring it to pass.*

Matthew 11: 28-30

> *Come unto me, all ye that labour and are heavy laden, and I will give you rest.*
> *Take my yoke upon you, and learn of me; for I am meek and lowly in heart: and ye shall find rest unto your souls.*
> *For my yoke is easy and my burden is light.*

♥♥♥♥♥♥♥

If you need a healing, you got it:

Isaiah 53: 4-5

> *Surely he hath borne our griefs, and carries our sorrows: yet we did esteem him striken, smitten of GOD, and afflicted.*

But he was wounded for our transgressions, he was Bruised for our iniquities: the chastisement of our Peace was upon him; and with his stripes we are healed.

Matthew 8: 16-17

When the even was come, they brought unto him many that were possessed with devils: and he cast the spirits with his word, and healed all that were sick.

That it might be fulfilled which was spoken by E-sá-ias the prophet, saying, Himself took our infirmities, and bare our sicknesses.

Mark 2: 10-11

But that ye may know that the Son of man hath power on earth to forgive sins (he saith to the sick of the palsy)

I say unto thee, Arise, and take up thy bed and go thy way into thine house.

Matthew 13: 15

FOR THIS PEOPLE'S HEART IS WAXED GROSS, AND THEIR EARS ARE DULL OF HEARING, AND THEIR EYES THEY HAVE CLOSED; LEST AT ANY TIME THEY SHOULD SEE WITH THEIR EYES, AND HEAR WITH THEIR EARS, AND SHOULD UNDERSTAND WITH THEIR HEART, AND SHOULD BE CONVERTED, AND I SHOULD HEAL THEM.

If you feel you will be judged, read:

Luke 6: 37

> *Judge not, and ye shall not be judge: condemn not, and ye shall not be condemned: forgive, and ye shall be forgiven.*

It is my belief that once you have changed, once you know that you will not do the things that you've once done, and once you are following the way of the righteous, do not allow others to remind you of the old you.

You did it. You acknowledged it. You paid the price. Now it is time to move on.

♥♥♥♥♥♥♥

If you need faith, turn to:

Matthew 17: 20

> *And, Jesus said unto them, Because of your unbelief: for verily I say unto you, If ye have faith as a grain of mustard seed, ye shall say unto this mountain, Remove hence to yonder place; and it shall remove; and nothing shall be impossible unto you.*

Mark 11: 22-26

> *And Jesus answering saith unto them, Have faith in GOD.*

*For verily I say unto you, That whoso-
ever shall say unto this mountain, Be thou removed and be thou cast into the sea; and shall
not doubt in his heart, but shall believe that
those things which he saith shall come to pass;
he shall have whatsoever he saith.*

*Therefore I say unto you, What things
soever ye desire, when ye pray, believe that
ye receive them, and ye shall have them.*

*And when ye stand praying, forgive, if ye
ought against any: that your Father also which is
in heaven may forgive you your trespasses.*

*But if ye do not forgive, neither will your
Father which is in heaven forgive your trespasses.*

Parents, you are not a mistake. Any and all things can be overcome. For GOD truly loves you. We love you. Such is the
power of AGAPE LOVE.

Choose now to get the spiritual and human help you
need. GOD has a plan for you. Consult GOD and find out your
plan.

Parents, stop neglecting your children.

6

Be encouraging; stop degrading your child

Actions and words can be uplifting or they can be degrading. Degrading words and actions cause humiliation. Experience has led me to conclude that people degrade other people with words more than any other means. When you call your child degrading names such as: stupid, big head, ugly, dog, b_ _ _ _, little m_ _ _ _ _ f _ _ _ _ _, heifer, dummy, nigger (nigga), etc., you are humiliating your child.

Degrading words attack moral and intellectual character. Degrading a child causes the child to lose self-esteem and self-respect. On the other hand, parents may want the opposite effects. Parents, you may really want your child to be intelligent, encouraged, and full of self-respect. You may really want your child to be successful in school and in life. However, the truth is, *parents, you are not going to get those results when you use degrading words; your child will become disrespectful to you and to others.*

Encouragement through words

Proverbs 10: 11

> *The mouth of a righteous man is a well of life: but violence covereth the mouth of the wicked.*

Were you ever called a name or talked to in such a way that you remember it as if it was yesterday?

Parents, what you say to your child has everlasting effects. Children are not great discriminators. They do not know what you really mean or 'that was then'.

Parents, you must **bless** and **edify** your child. Blessing your child means to respond with good words and to pray for your child. Edifying your child means to encourage your child. When you bless and edify your child, you love them in your voice, in the words that you speak, and in the tone in which you speak.

Proverbs 5: 4

> *A wholesome tongue is a tree of life: but perverseness therein is a breach in the spirit.*

Here are some encouraging words and phrases that one can use to build self-esteem and self-respect in children:

- ❖ You are a beautiful expression of divinity.
- ❖ You are much too intelligent/smart for that.
- ❖ Young lady/man
- ❖ Unique divine expression of GOD
- ❖ Smart/Intelligent

- ❖ My young intelligent son/daughter
- ❖ You are beautiful.
- ❖ The understanding will soon manifest; keep trying.
- ❖ I see greatness in you; you must see greatness in yourself.
- ❖ Pray.
- ❖ The only boundaries on you are the ones you set for yourself.
- ❖ All things are possible.
- ❖ Do it in Faith.
- ❖ Respect yourself. Remember, how you act and what you say show people how to treat you.

♥♥♥♥♥♥♥

Parents, as you establish and re-define your house rules, it is important to set guidelines for language and conversation that is acceptable within your home. You should consider the following:

- No teasing, talking about, or degrading anyone. No playing the 'Dozens'.
- Only constructive criticism is allowed. Constructive criticism must be accompanied with possible resolutions or helpful comments or gestures.
- Talking about a person is not how you debate an issue. You must defend your position with facts and/or examples.
- Do not use 'double negatives'. Use proper subject-verb agreement. You must use correct English..

- Repeated use of words means that you should employ the use of a thesaurus to find a synonym.

There is an added advantage for instituting an oral language policy in your home; you are enhancing oral language development. Some benefits include, but are not limited to, an increased vocabulary and a greater aptitude to describe things by using an assortment of words. In addition, there is an elevated ability to be understood by others.

Real case scenario #18

A student is suspended repeatedly for class disruption and verbal abuse. A Formal hearing is held. During the hearing, the verbal abuse violation is read aloud:

> *The student entered the class. When I, the teacher, asked the student to sit down, the student told me, "Shut the hell up." I told the student not to use inappropriate language, and the student replied, "I don't give a f _ _ _". I continued with my class, and the student continued to talk. I directed the student, "Ms. Jane, please be quiet." The student commented, "Kiss my a_ _, b_ _ _ _". I told the student to leave and go to the Assistant Principal's office, and I would send the referral and contact the parent.*

The administrator asked the teacher, "Mr. Smith, is there anything else?" The teacher stated, "When I contacted the parent, the mother said, 'Damn, all she did was curse'."

The mother interjected, "Everybody curses. S_ _ _!" The teacher and administrator turned to look at the mother. The mother did not appear to be the least bit embarrassed.

The child was found guilty and suspended.

Sadly, the mother's concern was not with the child's out of school suspension (OSS) and missing work. Additionally, there was a question as to whether the parent understood that the child's capability to succeed in school was being affected.

♥♥♥♥♥♥♥

Talking, cursing, and other forms of class disturbances are all too prevalent in classrooms across the country. Too many students believe that they have the right to do as they want in school and in the classroom, to the point where the educational process is impeded. Unfortunately, too many parents also support this cancerous behavior and contribute to the disruption in the classroom.

My belief:

Your child does not have the right to stop the educational process or hinder another child's education. Your child's right to an education ends when he/she interferes with another child's right to an education.

Encouragement through actions

Physical abusive actions, including corporal punishment, degrade and belittle. Yelling, hitting, punching, slapping, and kicking are just a few types of degrading actions causing humiliation and resulting in the loss of self-esteem and self-respect.

Many parents find it difficult to let go of these actions and behaviors, especially when such brutal procedures were used on them. An added defense is the self-belief of parents that they are better, behaviorally, because of being raised this way.

♥♥♥♥♥♥♥♥

Allow me to go off _{subject:}

Students in my class often have spoken about their parents being hypocrites. For example, a student stated that his parents told him not to use drugs, and he knew they had used them. He went on and on, and I listened. Then he asked me, "What do you think?"

(I thought about Jesus. Remember when Jesus was brought an adulterous woman? The people wanted to stone her based on the laws given to them by Moses. Jesus had to think about what to say and do. He did nothing and stated, " Let he who is without sin cast the first stone." The woman's life was spared.)

Returning to the question presented to me, I focused on parental love. I discussed how <u>times have changed</u>, and that the laws are different. I mentioned that when I was a teenager, no one asked for a drug test to work as a cashier. Nowadays, if you are caught with drugs in your car, the police will impound your car.

Getting back to the issues of degrading actions and corporal punishment, I want you to ask yourself these questions:

Question #1: Were you trying to teach or control your child when you used a degrading action?

Question #2: Were you trying to get your child to understand why what he/she had done was wrong, inappropriate, or unacceptable when you used corporal punishment?

Question #3: Were you upset that your child disobeyed you when you used corporal punishment?

Think.

Tradition can be hindering and sometimes interferes with the capability to recognize a better way of accomplishing a goal.

♥♥♥♥♥♥♥

Let us examine a real response to question #1:

Were you trying to teach or control your child when you used a degrading action?

The following setting is outlined in Real Case scenario #11.

The goal is to teach the child reading skills.
The parent is tired and yells at the child.
The child cries.
(Note: The child probably feels something is wrong. The child may even feel stupid.).

Now I ask you, *"Did yelling help the child to read?"*

No. What helped was the parent purchasing the appropriate materials and making the child feel relaxed, encouraged, and valued. The parent exhibiting patience with the child, expressing real care and concern, and rewarding the child all served to help the child learn to read.

However, yelling is a quicker, easier response. Parents, it is easy to degrade. It takes time to teach.

Proverbs 15: 7
The lips of the wise disperse knowledge: but the heart of the foolish doeth not so.

♥♥♥♥♥♥♥

Let us examine a possible response to question #2:

Were you trying to get your child to understand why what he/she had done was wrong, inappropriate, or unacceptable when you used corporal punishment?

Here, we will look at a common problem in society – theft. Stealing, embezzlement, armed robbery, and home invasion are all acts of theft.

A teacher calls a parent. The teacher informs the parent that she was notified by another student that her child took his calculator.

The mother searches her child's room and finds a watch. The mother questions her child about the watch. The child does not disclose from where she got the watch. The mother whips the child. Finally, the child states, "I found it."

Later that evening, a neighbor knocks on the door and tells the mother that her son's watch was missing after her child left their house. The mother asks the neighbor to describe the watch. The neighbor does, and the mother returns the watch. The mother commences to beating the child for lying and stealing.

The mother is satisfied with the punishment.

Now I ask you, "Do you think the child has learned that lying and stealing are wrong?

Think.

Parents, what would you do if this were your child?

Parents, write down everything you would do to teach your child that lying and stealing are wrong.

Parents, are you beginning to realize how much thought must go into teaching a child about wrongful, inappropriate, and unacceptable behaviors?

♥♥♥♥♥♥♥♥

Let us use the example in question #2 to examine question #3:

Were you upset that your child disobeyed you when you used corporal punishment?

If I believe that the mother had prior discussions with her child about stealing, one cannot disagree with me. Let us go one-step further. Let us say that the daughter disobeyed her mother's earlier directive – Do Not Steal. If this were the case, do you believe the mother used corporal punishment because the daughter disobeyed her?

Reflect.

♥♥♥♥♥♥♥♥

In real case scenario #27, a boy is struck by his mother's lover for refusing to do chores. This action contributed to the boy becoming more disobedient and disrespectful.

Parents, discipline means to teach, and as parents, we must learn to teach. Teaching is not quick nor is it easy. Teaching is time consuming. The most obvious means of teaching is to model the desired behaviors that you want to see in your child. Parents, learn to control <u>your</u> behaviors because your child will mirror <u>your</u> behaviors.

Parents, what actions and words are coming out of you, which defile you and your child?

Think.

Mark 7: 15 reads,

> *There is nothing from without a man that enter-ing into him can defile him: but the things which come out of him, those are they that defile the man.*

A synonym for defile is degrade. It is essential that we do not degrade through words or actions. As parents, your actions and words need to be uplifting, encouraging, loving, under-standing, respectful, motivational, instructional, patient, inspira-tional, moving, trustful, faithful, etc.

Parents, when you hit, your child learns to hit. When you are violent, your child learns to be violent. When you de-grade, your child learns to degrade. When you criticize, your child learns to be critical.

Parents, do not degrade or belittle your child. Keep in mind that such actions may cause a child to lose self-esteem and self-respect.

Remember parents, <u>You</u> are the Power behind your Child's Success.

♥♥♥♥♥♥♥♥

Colossians 3: 21

> *Fathers, provoke not your children to anger, lest they be discouraged.*

Parents, there are other ways to discipline without angering your child, but I guarantee that when you discipline in love, you will not anger your child. Parents, when you love, your child loves. When you encourage your child, your child is encouraged. When you respect your child, your child respects you and others. Parents, when you demonstrate loving, encouraging words and actions, you are nurturing your child's potential.

Parents, you are the Power behind your Child's Success.

♥♥♥♥♥♥♥♥

Proverbs 15: 1

> *A soft answer turneth away wrath: but grievous words stir up anger.*

Proverbs 18:21

> *Death and Life are in the power of the tongue: and they that love it shall eat the fruit thereof.*

Parents, exhibit encouraging behavior and speak encouraging words that help your child succeed in life.

7

Protecting your child

A child's health is based on his/her mental, physical, and emotional well-being. The strengthening and preservation of these states must be protected. Any type of tradition, action, or habit, which creates an abusive or neglectful situation for your child, must be eradicated from your child's environment.

Statistics on Child abuse and neglect are underestimated in America due to non-reported incidents. As an educator, school social workers informed me that more abuse takes place after 5 p.m. than any other time. Possible reasons for this time-line include, but are not limited to, children being left alone after school, parents' work related stresses, and the mail (reminding parents of overburdening responsibilities, bills, and other financial obligations).

If parents are not able to captivate their emotions, the pressure caused by these aforementioned factors could very well invite neglect and abuse in the home. When this happens, the child's security blanket is torn, the child's safety shield is fractured, and the child becomes a direct object of harm.

Real case scenario #19

A student was getting into a lot of trouble. The teacher brought the 8-year-old student to an administrator after she tried numerous times to get in touch with a parent. The administrator got a contact number from the student's sister. He dialed the phone number. The administrator was informed that the phone number was that of a neighbor. The former neighbor told the administrator that she was unaware of the whereabouts and the living conditions of the student, and that he should try to call the stepfather.

The administrator called who he had been told was the stepfather. The man on the phone stated to the administrator that he only played the role of the stepfather. He said, "I'm involved with the mother of the student. We have a two-year-old child together, and in all honesty, I haven't seen the mother for two weeks." He added, "I was diagnosed with cancer, and I have been unable to work.

Reader, what do you think the child was going through if the parents could not positively manage their stressful situations?

Could the child have felt the stress in the home and acted out?

Think.

Parents, the transfer of stress from parent to child is very real. Emotional harm is as damaging as physical harm. Protection includes getting the child, and sometimes the entire family, the help to cope with life changing situations.

In this real case scenario, one can conclude that the form of protection warranted was protection from the parents. This 8-year-old child needed protection from the very persons charged with caring for her.

♥♥♥♥♥♥♥♥

I will never forget when a student approached me to inquire about a group project. His sleeves were slightly rolled, and I could see part of his forearm. There were numerous scars on his arm, about three centimeters in length.

When he left my desk, I went straight to the counselor. I told the counselor about the student. The name was familiar to her. She stated that the student's parents were going through a very acrimonious, verbally abusive divorce and custody battle. She added that the young man became so emotionally distraught that he started cutting himself with razor blades.

The next day, when I arrived at school, I went next door to speak with a senior colleague. I wanted to know if she had ever come across a student who she believed to be inflicting self-harm. Her response, much to my astonishment, was yes.

Real case scenario #20

A teacher overhears a conversation between students. A 17-year-age female student is heard saying, "I ride the trains until about midnight, then I go home."

Before the end of the class, the teacher initiates a conversation, which leads to asking the student, "Why do you ride the trains late at night?" The student replies, "My mother's boyfriend tries to mess with me. He keeps touching me and mak-

ing advances. When I told my mother, she said I was lying. Since I don't have any place to stay, I ride the trains until I know they are asleep, and I try to wake up before them."

This real case scenario shows the need to move beyond personal interests to protect children. As well, it also reminds one that older children too need protection.

♥♥♥♥♥♥♥

Let us examine the word *harm*. To harm means to hurt, to damage, to injure, and to impair. Harm does not always mean to commit physical injury. As stated earlier, one can commit emotional harm.

Whether one believes that one has harmed is subjective. Therefore, if one believes that one has not harmed, then one finds no need to help or protect.

Bruises and physical injuries can cause one to identify harm and the need to help and protect. In addition, inappropriate behavior, in the form of words and actions, can cause one to identify harm and the need to help and protect. A more elusive form of harm is the perception of harm. The perception of being harmed is real harm.

In other words, *"perception is real"*. If a child believes he/she has been harmed, frankly speaking, he/she has been harmed. Ponder on this while I interject an analogous situation centering on bullying.

Real case scenario #21
A black male student with a 3.7 GPA enters a predominantly white classroom in which he has the highest-class average. He

sits down, and a group of white students enters the classroom and congregates around him.

A white male student asks, "Do you want to hear a joke?"

Several peers in the group simultaneously reply, "Yes."

The student asks, "What do you call a Black Man wearing a suit?"

(No one responds.)

He then states the answer, "Defendant."

(The students laugh.)

The young man continues, "What do you say to a Black Man wearing a suit?"

(No one responds.)

"Defendant, will you please rise," he replies.

(The crowd laughs.)

The black male student informs the teacher, who does nothing. The next day, the student walks in then out of the classroom. The student goes to inform an administrator.

The administrator recognizes that what had occurred was 'Bullying.'

Parents, how many children are emotionally harmed, every day, because of bullying?

Think.

There are many forms of bullying, both physical and non-physical. Words, gestures, songs, jokes, and drawings are just some non-physical forms of bullying. They do not leave scars on the skin.

141

Bullying is a means of intimidating and creating a threatening environment. If a person feels intimidated or if a person feels threatened, then that person has been bullied. Keep in mind, it is not what the perpetrator intended, it is how the victim feels.

Reflecting back
In real case scenario #20, the young lady was definitely emotionally harmed, and as a result, needed help and protection. The mother clearly failed to help and protect her daughter. Feeling dejected, the young lady attempts to help and protect herself. With no place to go, the daughter stays out at night to avoid the threatening environment, and exchanges one threatening environment for another.

Parents, remember that perception <u>is</u> reality.

♥♥♥♥♥♥♥

There are five '***human** must haves*' one needs to help and protect a child:

LOVE   **OPENNESS**   **EMPATHY**

SUPPORT   **RESOURCES**

LOVE – Parents, you must show affection and devotion towards your child.

OPENNESS – Parents, you must be open and receptive to learning and communicating with your child.

Parents, you must be aware of people, places, and things that are not in your child's best interest, which have the perception and potential to be harmful.

EMPATHY – Parents, you must place yourself in your child's shoes, and try to understand and feel what she/he is experiencing.

SUPPORT - Parents, you must bear the burden of your child's pain when harm does occur, and uphold your child's value.

RESOURCES – Parents, you must locate, identify, and use resources that will prevent, help, and protect your child both from harm and after harm.

♥♥♥♥♥♥♥

Real Case Scenario 22

A middle class family, living the American Dream in a very nice house, has two daughters. The family belongs to one of the Mega Churches in the area. Family pictures adorn the walls. Holiday meals are attended by relatives and produce post card memories.

One day, the 14 year age daughter walks to the mail box, never to return as the naive youth that she is. For more than seven years, she is exploited as a teen prostitute.

The mother discloses to me that this was not a kidnapping or child abduction. She states, " I later learned that the friends my daughter was associating with from her middle school, were recruiting her into prostitution. They convinced my daughter to meet them, and my daughter was gone."

She continued, "Later, I had learned about the sex acts

going on in the schools. I learned that many pimps are teenage boys and girls. Also, I learned how little is done to stop teenage prostitution by many police departments and other authorities.

Statistic 7:
According to a study by Estes and Weiner, "Child sexual exploitation is the most hidden form of child abuse in the U.S. and North America today. It is the nation's least recognize epidemic." The study estimates that over 300,000 children a year are subject to sexual exploitation in the U.S.

What is so shocking about the Real case scenario you just read?

Well, the 14 year age girl does not fit into the top three categories of children entering into the sex trade industry: runaways, thrownaways (children thrown out of their homes), and homeless children.

♥♥♥♥♥♥♥

Parents, let me tell you about two other shocking incidents.

Incident #1:
A mother receives a phone call from her brother. The brother tells the mother to go to You Tube to view a video. The video is that of the mother's daughter, the brother's niece. The daughter had made a video using a cell phone in the comforts of her own bedroom. The brother's daughter informed him of the video that the cousin had made. The mother and brother were both amazed and enlightened on how out of touch they were with the capabilities of technology, uploading a video to the internet using a simple cell phone.

Incident #2:

A 16 year age girl received international attention when she traveled to the middle east to rendezvous with a 20 year age young man. She met the young man on the internet. The girl was corresponding with the young man for 2 years through a MySpace Account. Her parents never knew it.

Parents, know with whom your child associates.

♥♥♥♥♥♥♥♥

Parents, if you are spiritual or moving towards spirituality, then an understanding of GOD's divine presence and power are necessary. Enter into prayer and a covenant with GOD. Let GOD move in and through you. Learn when GOD is speaking to you. Let GOD order your words and actions. Parents, GOD will provide a shield of protection for you and your family that is impermeable.

Real Case Scenario 23

A young woman, who is cohabitating with one of her children's fathers, takes on a part time job. The couple is going through financial difficulties due to the father's crack addiction.

One evening, while at work, the woman gets up from her desk and gathers her belongings. The woman tells a co-worker that she needs to go home. She states, "Spirit is telling me to go home."

Upon her arrival at the house, she notices a very anxious father. The young lady discloses to me that spirit told her never

145

again to leave her children alone with him. The young mother states, "I don't know what was avoided, but I know that GOD prevented something bad form happening, and my obedience to GOD protected my children from harm"

Several months later, the young mother left the father. In speaking with her, she said, "Spirit told me to leave, and I left."

Conversations

I remember two conversations I had with very close friends.

Conversation #1:

A close friend revealed to me how she had been raped by an evil spirit in her house. She stated that after she let her male friend moved in, a feeling of dissonance entered her home. She said that she never felt safe or at peace since he had been living there. She continued, "When I heard GOD's spirit speak to me, telling me to get rid of him, that's exactly what I did. Now, I feel safe and at peace again."

Conversation #2:

As my friend and I discussed married life, children, husbands, and wives, we started laughing. Both of us had disclosed the deciding factor for marrying our husbands. My friend and I talked about how spirit guided our choice to married someone who would protect his family through love and seek wisdom to make decisions.

Psalms 115: 11

*Ye that fear the Lord, trust in the Lord: he **is** their help and shield.*

Parents, protect your children.

PART III

PARENTS, BE THE RESPONSIBLE ADULT

8

Your purpose, your position

Being comfortable in your parent role

❖ Parents, how do you feel in your role as a parent?

❖ Parents, do you feel that you lack important knowledge and information?

❖ Parents, are you puzzled at times about what to do?

❖ Parents, are you confused and indecisive?

❖ Parents, are you overwhelmed?

❖ Parents, do you stick your head in the sand and hope tomorrow will be a better day?

❖ Parents, are you optimistic?

❖ Parents, are you taking care of your child?

❖ Parents, are you taking care of yourself?

Proverbs 23:24

>   *The father of the righteous shall greatly rejoice: and he that begetteth a wise child shall have joy of him.*

Parents, your purpose is to develop a child who is wise and educated .

Parents, it is important that you know your purpose as a parent. You must feel comfortable in your position as a parent. From time to time, your child will test your parental role.

Example:

>   A single parent informed me about the time she told her children that this was going to be a *'clean-up the house day'*. The children responded, "We want to go with DAD. We have fun with DAD."
>
>   The mother quickly replied, "But you eat with me." She added, "My job is to keep food in your belly, clothes on your back, a roof over your head, make sure you get a good education, and send you off to college, so you can become a responsible and successful adult."

This mother truly knows her purpose.

Parents, the best reared, raised, and behaved child will test you. Many parents have stated to me that they had no problems with their child during elementary and middle schools. However, once their child was in high school, there was an onset of issues. Some of these parents would question themselves, asking, "What happened? What did I do wrong?"

Sometimes, I would just sit and listen because the record showed that such reactions from parents were dramatic. Surprisingly, the majority of parents who generated these responses were actually honest in their convictions. Still, these parents were often embarrassed or in a state of disbelief when the challenges came.

There were times when I would console them with a truth about kids. I would tell them, "*I have been an educator for over ten years, and believe me; the best reared, raised, and behaved children will test their parents. It usually happens during the teenage years. It has something to do with being a teenager.*"

To be honest, many challenges arise during the teenage years, and even the best parent has no immunity from a teenager's test. There are many reasons why a child may test a parent. Some reasons are *to get attention, to see if the parent is concerned,* and *simply to see if the parent cares.*

Parents, you must be able to recognize any test and respond fairly, responsibly, and with compassion. Recognition of a test is going to be based on you knowing your child. Parents, if you do not know what is right and normal with your child, you will not be able to distinguish when something is wrong or abnormal. Communicating with your child and paying attention to verbal as well as non-verbal clues will aid you in learning and knowing your child. (Review chapter 4 – **Communication**)

Parents, at times, the test is small and seems insignificant, such as a missed chore. Other times, the test may be major but so subtle that it goes unnoticed, such as experimenting with drugs, sex, or an abusive relationship. Your child may appear to be fine on the surface, but in reality, your child may be feeling depressed, pressured, or inadequate.

Parents, when your child tests you, you must respond, <u>never ignore</u>.

♥♥♥♥♥♥♥

A subtle test requires a subtle response.

Example:

> Your child neglects a chore.
> Your response may be a brief statement, such as *"John, I noticed that the floor has not been mopped."*

Wait for a response and proceed accordingly.

♥♥♥♥♥♥♥

An overt test requires an overt response.

Example:

> You find a note indicating that your child is having sex. Your response may be to go to a Medical bookstore and purchase the book

with the most graphic sexual diseased pictures in it. You want pictures that show chancre sores, holes in the penis and vagina, and warts all over the sexual organs that look like mountains. The pictures that would make you stop having sex are the best ones.

Next, go to the copy store and make 8" x 10" color copies. Arrange the pictures in order from least dramatic to the ones that make you vomit or at least sick to the stomach.

Then, prepare a nice loving meal for your child. After dinner, initiate a conversation about sex speaking in third party format. Just say, "It seems like every movie, on television, shows people having sex with no apparent consequences."

Subsequently, ask your child what he/she thinks. Wait for a response and proceed accordingly. By this time, you may want to serve your child dessert.

Eventually, you will show and explain the pictures to your child. Try not to lecture, at least not yet.

I think you can take it from here. Parents, if you have selected the right pictures, your child should start crossing his/her legs, turning his/her head, or throwing up towards the end of the presentation.

If or when you lecture, express care and concern, and tap into your child's strengths, uniqueness, greatness, and goals in life. More importantly, do more listening than talking.

Parents, is not this teaching/discipline method better than beating, yelling, or punishing?

Note that this method is not quick or easy.

♥♥♥♥♥♥♥♥

Whether it is the most subtle or most overt test, there are rules to responding:

    Rule 1: Do not react.
    Rule 2: Be calm, cool, and collect yourself.
    Rule 3: Think about the outcomes you want for your child (accept responsibility, never engage in this practice again, think about the possible effects of the behavior, what could happen if you were an adult, how will this affect your life plans, the hindering effects, etc.).
    Rule 4: Write down the risks of your plan (including safety hazards to your child).
    Rule 5: Write down your child's possible reactions and responses.
    Rule 6: Give proper notification to appropriate individuals.
    Rule 7: Discuss the plan with appropriate individuals.
    Rule 8: Write down any personal consequences if your plan fails.

Based on my experience as a mother and learning from others, when your child tests you, you must out think him/her. Sometimes you must use the '***ultimate out-thinking eye-opening to teach your child a lesson he/she will never forget***' consequential response.

Real case scenario #24

Several hours after dropping off his freshman son at school, a father receives a phone call from the assistant principal (AP). The AP asks, "Does your child have an electronic organizer?"

Father: *Yes.*

AP: *Does he have two?*

Father: *No.*

AP: *He claims that one belongs to his mother.*

Father: *OK. His mother does have one. What's the issue?*

AP: *Your son was trying to sell an electronic organizer in school. Solicitation in school is not allowed.*

Father: *I'm on my way.*

(While on his way to the school, the father calls his wife and finds out that she is in possession of her electronic organizer.)

Mother: *Why do you ask?*

Father: *Our son is in possession of two electronic organizers. He was trying to sell one; that's solicitation. The assistant principal called me, and I'm on my way to the school. (The father was in the assistant principal's office within twenty minutes.)*

AP: *John was trying to sell an electronic organizer to students.*

Father: *What are your thoughts?*

AP: *Well, there's no solicitation in school. A teacher brought the incident to my attention. I need to find out to whom the elec-*

tronic organizer belongs and if it's stolen.

Father: *Where are you in your investigation?*

AP: *After checking with students in your son's first and second period classes, no one is missing an electronic organizer.*

    (It is the beginning of third period.)

Father: *OK, let's get to the bottom of this.*

The father goes into the other room and with a calm, cool, friendly look and voice asks, "Hello, how's school? (No response, just the look of shock, puzzlement, and fear) Why am I here?"

Son: *I found an electronic organizer in first period as I was leaving, and instead of turning it in, well, I was going to turn it in, I decided to keep it. Then, I decided to sell it and make some money. (The father gave him "the look". He continued.)*

  A teacher overheard me trying to sell the electronic organizer and called the assistant principal. The assistant principal brought me to her office and said that it was against school rules to sell anything in school. She then asked, "John, where did you get the electronic organizer?" I replied, "From my mom."

Father: *OK, I'll be right back.*

(The father left, called his wife, and tried to calm himself, which took about ten minutes. The father went back into the AP's office and sat in the chair.)

AP: *What did John say?*

Father: *(The father told her exactly what his son had stated to him. After a brief silence, he continued.)*

Yes, this is definitely solicitation, and with every day that passes, the chances of knowing where the electronic organizer came from, decrease. Therefore, the discipline he receives needs to teach him that his actions could be considered theft. Even if the owner is not established, he cannot prove that he found the electronic organizer.

(The father asks the AP if he can handle this situation in lieu of any consequences based on solicitation while she continues to look for the owner. In addition, he asks the AP if she can follow along with what he is about to do. She is somewhat hesitant but agrees. The father summons the son into the AP's office.)

Father: *Young man, take a seat. (The father turns to the son.) This is bad, very bad. (Pause) You broke the school's Solicitation rule. In addition, you have given conflicting stories about the origin of the electronic organizer. Is this correct?*
Son: *Yes.*
Father: *Now, we know the electronic organizer didn't come from home. (Pause) More importantly, you can't prove that you found it.*
Son: *I did find it.*
Father: *I never said that you didn't find it. I said that you could not prove it. Let me present to you a hypothetical scenario. Suppose a friend of yours finds a gold chain. He sells it to you. You purchase it. You wear it to school. Another student notices you wearing his chain, and declares, "You stole it from me". He has proof that it's his chain because his initials are engraved in it. You look and find the initials. An administrator intervenes, and you have to give the chain back. What's worse, your friend claims he did not sell it to you. You have no receipt, no*

159

eyewitness, and no proof of the sale. You're out of fifty dollars, and people think you are a thief.

Son: *I would be so mad at my friend and probably want to harm him.*

Father: *OK, you provoke a fight, and you are suspended from school for ten days. Your friend's mother files charges against you for physical assault. You are found guilty and receive probation. You see, your actions have consequences. (The assistant principal nods.) Do you understand?*

Son: *Yes.*

Father: *Repeat what I just said to you.*

(The son repeats it.)

Father: *John, stand up. Give me your transit card.*

Son: *How will I get home?*

Father: *That's a difficult choice, and I hope you choose correctly. What I want you to understand is that your actions can result in unpredictable consequences that can place you in a vulnerable situation. Do you have your house keys?*

Son: *Yes.*

Father: *Good. Well, go back to class, and I will see you at home. Son, I love you, and want you to make the right choices.*

(The son exits the room, and the father continues speaking with the AP.)

Father: *My son is hardheaded, but he has common sense. More than likely, he will call his mother to pick him up.*

AP: *Does he know we have school buses to transport him near his house?*

Father: *No, but if he doesn't call his mother, he'll play the 'I* *have no way home' card to get you involved. So, if you could instruct him on how to get home or call me if the buses have left, I would appreciate it. I will continue with the lesson at home and let you know the outcome.*

(Instead of returning to work, the father goes home and calls his wife to inform her of the series of events. The two carefully plan their next move. It is decided that the mother should leave work early and position herself several miles from the school.)

(The son enters the house around 5pm.)

Father: *Good, you made it home. Let's step outside. How did you get home?*

Son: *Well, I started walking and realized that I didn't know the way home. I was confused and tired, so I decided to call DAD. He picked me up and brought me home.*

Father: *He didn't stay?*

Son: *No.*

Father: *Wait right here. I need to call your mother and tell her that you're home.*

(The father goes inside the house and calls the mother. He informs his wife of the series of events. They decide that it would be best for her to call the son's biological father for information about any possible dialogue during the ride home. In addition, the father is to take the son's keys and discuss responsibility.)

♥♥♥♥♥♥♥

Mother: *Hello.*

Biological Father: *Hey! John told me what happened.*

Mother: *You know about the two electronic organizers and that he tried to sell one?*

Biological Father: *Yes, he told me, and I told him that one could easily conclude that he might have stolen the electronic organizer.*

Mother: *Good. So we're on the same page?*

Biological Father: *Definitely. Let me know what you decide.*

Mother: *OK. Bye.*

♥♥♥♥♥♥♥

Father: *Son, take a seat. Your mother and I feel that you don't understand the value of trust, and how it affects people believing that you are responsible. We have to trust you and trust that you can handle responsibility. Do you understand?*

Son: *Yes.*

Father: *Now, we will supply your needs - without a doubt, but the more trust you earn, the more responsibilities you get. The more responsibilities you can manage, the more wants you get-period. John, I'm going to be very frank with you. If we allow or condone inappropriate behavior, we will be setting you up for a life of jail, death, or poverty. Now, you have 24 hours to decide about the type of life you want and how to get it. You also need to think about what type of life you will have if you make choices that will place you in jail or living in poverty. To bring this point home, you must turn over your door keys. (John looked astonished.)* **Turn over your door keys.** *(John relinquished the door keys.) Wait out here until your mother comes home. She should be here in about twenty minutes.*

Son: *Why are you taking my door keys?*

Father: *Well, having door keys means you are mature enough to manage the responsibility of having access to the home, even when we are not at home. We must trust you to use wisdom, discernment, and discretion about the people, things, behavior, and actions that you allow to take place in this house. Also, we must trust you to be able to understand the possible effects of your choices.*

♥♥♥♥♥♥♥

(The mother pulls into the driveway. The mother gets out of the car and walks over to the son.)

Mother: *Hello, son.*

Son: *Hello, mom. (Stated in a depressing voice)*

Mother: *You know we love you. (The boy nodded.) Needless to say, we are disappointed. I'll be back. (The mother enters the house and makes herself a cup of coffee. The father enters a short time later. The mother smiles at the father.)*

♥♥♥♥♥♥♥

Mother: *How are we doing?*

Father: *Good. He's definitely in shock about how we're handling the matter.*

Mother: *How do you feel about him calling his biological father?*

Father: *Well, I'm a little disappointed. I never expected that. Putting myself in his shoes, I probably would have tried to show my parents I had alternatives. What did he say?*

163

Mother: *Well, he mentioned to John about how one could easily consider him a thief.*

Father: *Good.*

Mother: *Time for me to take over.*

Father: *Go for it.*

♥♥♥♥♥♥♥♥

Mother: *(The mother allows the son to enter the house. The mother sits down at the dining table and tells the son to take a seat.) How's your day going so far? (John shakes his head.) What a difference a day makes. This morning you had trust and unlimited access to the house. Now, you have to earn back the trust to get back the keys. This morning the AP didn't know you. Now, her first encounter with you probably gives her a negative perception of you. This morning you knew you were going to come home to a good meal. Now, you will have bread and wa-ter, only. (John shook his head again.) This morning you had a bed in which to sleep. Now, you will sleep on the hardwood liv-ing room floor, and regardless of how unfair or extreme you may think we are, in court, you would be unable to prove that you found the electronic organizer, and probably be convicted of theft. Get the picture?*

Son: *Yes.*

(The next morning, the father takes his son to school and returns the transit card to him. The father goes inside to speak with the AP. The AP informs the father that they cannot determine the owner of the electronic organizer. The father enlightens the AP on yesterday's series of events. The AP determines that the

parents' handling of the situation was much worse than the After School Detention the child would have served for the solicitation infraction. In addition, the AP feels that the question of theft has been dealt with even though the school had no evidence. The AP thanks the father for coming to school, and working with the school on this matter.)

Update: *One other disciplinary action occurred, teasing, during John's sophomore year. At the time this book was written, John had a 3.67 GPA. He was taking an AP class and did score over 1200* on the SAT (in his first attempt). (*Maximum SAT score at the time was 1600).*

♥♥♥♥♥♥♥♥

Parents, think about how you would have answered the following questions prior to reading this real case scenario.

> *How many parents would have resorted to Corporal punishment?*

> *Would that have been an effective resolution?*

Let me reiterate, corporal punishment is mindless, easy to do, and requires little time. It teaches physical strength and violence. A child will learn to value physical strength and violence from corporal punishment. However, most parents do not want to teach their child how to abuse physical strength or act violently.

Parents, the desired outcome requires the correct teaching strategy (rod/reproof) not the easiest or most comfortable one.

Proverbs 29:15

> *The rod and reproof give <u>wisdom</u>: but a child left to him self bringeth his mother to shame.*

♥♥♥♥♥♥♥♥

Once a parent asked me, "What should I do?" She said, "My child is turning into a disrespectful, rude individual." I responded with a question, "What do you think? She answered, "I need to find out what is going on in his head."

I applauded her for her honesty. Quite often, parents do not have enough information to discipline/teach their child correctly. Parents may need to search their child's room. For additional information, parents may need to consult with their child's teachers regarding changes in their child's work or attitude.

I suggested that she take him to dinner, ask leading questions, and just listen. Sometimes, a simple loving act will be enough to reposition a child back on track.

I reaffirmed that whatever she decided to do, she needed to emphasize his value, uniqueness, and successes. I admitted that I did not know her child, and that she knew more than I did. I also said that if she felt safety, violence, suicidal tendencies, or severe depression may be involved, she needed to seek professional help immediately.

Parents, do not second-guess teenage depression.

♥♥♥♥♥♥♥♥

Parent's roles

A parent must perform several roles. Parents must assume the roles of caretaker and teacher. These roles will be discussed in this section. After discussing the caretaker and teacher roles, if you feel uncomfortable or unsure about your performance in these roles, GET HELP. This is not the time to be *super- mom* or *super-dad.* Always remember that it is not about you, it is about your child.

The parent's caretaker role

As a caretaker, there are everyday responsibilities you are required to perform. These duties can be categorized based on priority. The survival list, the needs list, and the wants list make up the three categories. These categories will be used to emphasize the caretaker's role.

I introduced these three lists in chapter six. As a caretaker, you are required to meet the provisions on the survival and needs lists, not the wants list. Many parents are astounded when I express that the wants list is not mandatory for success in school or in life. In chapter 6, the needs list included quality time for nurturance, and the wants list included a luxury car. The wants list could have just as well registered a car for the child.

As a parent, if you meet the survival list and wants list without meeting the needs list, you may create a child who has everything (materialistically speaking). However, in addition to having everything, that child may have poor grades, low self-esteem, low self-respect, and have a tendency to be a follower.

♥♥♥♥♥♥♥

Let us revisit some items that you will find on a survival list. These items include food, shelter, clothing, safe environment, and basic health care. Sorry to say, many parents are not meeting their responsibilities as caretakers. They are not meeting their child's basic survival needs.

Real case scenario #25

My first three years of teaching were spent trying to understand the excuses parents gave for not meeting their child's survival needs.

When I spoke, many of my colleagues believed that I grew up middle class and in the suburbs. Actually, I grew up on the Westside of Chicago under the watchful eyes of family, friends, and neighbors. I attended public schools, including a college prep high school. Because I had a speech impediment, I met with a speech pathologist and took speech lessons. I was part of a drama guild. On Saturdays, my brother and I rode the train downtown to the Fine Arts building where we took piano lessons. As a member of the youth group at church, I went on summer retreats where I would spend one week on a college campus. In addition, I participated in a cotillion, I learned karate, went to camp, went on family vacations, and traveled with my mother to bowling tournaments.

I remember coming home during the summer break after

my first year of college. I saw my mother's check stub. I gasped, and I called my sister. I asked, "Are we poor?" My sister responded, "Yes, poor and privileged."

At that moment, my brain went into total rewind. We (five siblings including self) were never on public assistance, had private health care, and were protected by my mother's wisdom, strength, and nurturance. I grew up thinking beans were a substitute for meat. We made syrup from maple flavoring and milk from dry milk. All ice cream and desserts were homemade. My mother sewed and made the majority of our clothes. One time attire for plays, uniforms and costumes, usually was purchased as second hand items. First quality clothing required a trip to Marshall Fields, Florshiem shoes, or Hanns shoes.

I grew up during a time when nearly every household was a micro-economy. My mother and aunts sewed, my mother's cousins and my father repaired cars, my brothers got their hair cut at a neighbor's house, a man came to pick up and drop off the dry cleaning, and the doctor came to visit.

My mother helped others, and she was aided by family and friends. In addition, my mother actively was involved in the PTA and community organizations.

I was the product of divorced parents, and my father did contribute. I thought my mother and father were the best of friends until that revealing summer. My eyes were opened; I had been protected from the acrimony that existed between them, and I was allowed to grow up in a child's world.

I thank my mother.

♥♥♥♥♥♥♥

As an adult, I know my mother has a covenant with GOD. As an adult, I realize that our survival provisions and needs were met. Instead of meat on the table, we participated in activities that helped us to reach our full potential. Instead of expensive clothing, we had a grand piano. Instead of my mother allowing us to hang-out, my mother made sure that we received a quality education. Instead of going to the general high school, my mother paid for transportation to the public college prep high school across town. My mother could have continued working at the post office where she made good money, but she left to work at the Social Security Administration. The pay was less, but there was more time to nurture us. My mother's choices encouraged and contributed to the enhancement of our self-esteem and self-respect. Her wisdom, strength, and nurturance countered peer pressure and the effects of being teased by other children.

I received an average of two toys for Christmas even though I submitted a **'wants list'** of 50 items. I wanted a car, did not get that either. I wanted to go to parties; I think I went to three. I wanted to run away from home. I did not do it because it was too cold, and my mother made it mandatory for us to use common sense, so I ran away to college.

After meeting and comparing myself to others, I realize how blessed I was. According to America, we were discounted, but because of my mother's choices, we moved from low income to middle class, and we were privileged.

♥♥♥♥♥♥♥

Parents, YOU are the POWER behind your Child's Success.

♥♥♥♥♥♥♥♥

Developing a needs list is not easy. A needs list is subjective and open ended. It is what I call a working needs list. The more caretakers are involved, the more compromising or subjective a needs list becomes.

Some items you will find on a needs list are love, encouragement, a 'safe, quality learning environment', and a sense of belonging. Subjectivity enters in accordance to the means by which to provide these items.

Your list may be specific, such as:

- Transportation costs for school
- Save $10,000 per year
- Daily hugs
- Family time

If your child is having difficulty in school, you may add:

✓ Tutoring
✓ Math software

If your child is being bullied in school, you may add:

✓ Self defense class
✓ Change of school/tuition cost

171

In addition, your needs list should include materials that aid you in your role as a teacher.

The parent's teacher role

As a parent, you have been entrusted to teach your child the knowledge and conduct that will help him/her to succeed in life. Parents, a realistic, quality set of values must be practiced in your home and instilled in your child.

Values can vary from family to family because values are determined by a multiplicity of dynamics such as culture, history, and socioeconomic conditions. However, some essential values must be instilled in <u>all</u> children. They are respect, responsibility, character, and integrity. Parents, you must teach your child these values. In addition, your child must learn to distinguish between perception and reality.

Teaching respect, responsibility, character, and integrity

Parents, there are ways to develop your teaching skills. Children learn by seeing, hearing, reading, writing, explaining, doing, and repeating. Every teaching method should be based on how children learn. I will introduce you to a few simple, practical, 'easy to do' teaching and assessment methods.

Teaching methods:

1. DEMONSTRATE – Be a living example to your child. Demonstrate behaviors that you want your child to model. Therefore, be respectful, responsible, and a person of character and integrity. Demonstrate these behaviors at all times. No hypocrisy.

2. SPEAK – Speak respectfully, speak responsibly, speak with character, and speak with integrity. Your language must <u>not</u> be disrespectful, irresponsible, degrading, or humiliating.

3. SHOW – Show your child other living examples. Have them meet respectable, responsible people of character and integrity. Attend speaking engagements.

4. READ – Have your child read about these qualities and discuss people who exhibit these qualities.

5. WRITE – Have your child write about these qualities and describe people who exhibit these qualities.

6. EXPLAIN – Explain what these qualities are and their values. Show linkage. For example, responsibility leads to trust, which leads to certain liberties and rewards (refer to real case scenario #24).

7. EXHIBIT – Have your child demonstrate these qualities at all times.

8. REPEAT - Repeat teaching strategies 1-7 at all times.

Assessment methods:

1. MONITOR – Observe what your child does.

2. DIALOGUE – Talk to your child to assess knowledge and understanding.

3. SCRUTINIZE – Examine and analyze your child's knowledge, understanding, and actions to make sure they are responsible, respectable, exhibit character, and demonstrate integrity.

Parents, you must teach your child respect. You must teach your child responsibility. You must teach your child character. You must teach your child integrity. Parents, your child must learn and possess respect, responsibility, character, and integrity. Parents, your child must demonstrate these values all the time. In reality, there can never be undemonstrated knowledge.

Real case scenario #26
A videotaped hazing activity involving students at an Illinois high school, gained international attention. Televised video of the event, held in a park, showed senior girls covering junior girls with mud, paint, feces, and garbage, as onlookers, some hoisting beer cups, cheered.

The school district expelled 33 seniors and disciplined 20 juniors. Sixteen of the students were convicted of misdemeanor battery or alcohol charges. Two mothers were convicted of providing alcohol to minors.

With devastating repercussions, several parents watched as their children were allowed to act irresponsibly, disrespecting others in the name of so-called *"harmless fun"*.

The knowledge of knowing better means the responsibility of doing better. *A respectful, responsible adult with character and integrity must start with a respectful responsible child with character and integrity.*

Parents, never allow for 'undemonstrated understanding'.

♥♥♥♥♥♥♥♥

Respect, responsibility, character, and integrity are qualities that enhance education in the classroom. A respectful and responsible student will always be more welcomed in a class. A teacher will make extra time to help this type of student.

Every day, thousands of teachers are disrespected. There is very little extra help for rude students. Remember, a teacher can choose who he/she wants to help outside of school hours, who he/she wants to write a recommendation for, and who he/she allows to use his/her name as a reference.

In order to work in today's schools with today's students, the most effective teachers must:

1) use their personal salary to supply materials outside of the school's resources
2) stay longer than their scheduled hours
3) be a motivator
4) be willing to contact parents during off job hours

Hint #2

You never want teachers just to do their job.

A child who is so disrespectful, rude, verbally abusive, and out of control, will quickly be relegated to an alternative

175

educational setting because of liability issues and the school climate. In an alternative setting, the parent's options are very limited.

Hint #3

When you are tired of dealing with your rude, disrespectful, verbally abusive, and out of control child, the school is tired too.

Parents, remember that in order for a child to succeed in school, a child must be in school.

♥♥♥♥♥♥♥♥

Hint #4

If your child comes home and says, "The teacher disrespected me...", more than likely, your child doesn't know how to be respectful or even knows what respect is.

Why? Here is the answer. Teachers are trained to use a series of increasing directives. For example, my pattern of directives is:

> **First** - Young intelligent people please pay attention.
> **Second** – Young intelligent people (pause) please be quiet. (Slightly louder)
> **Third** – Young intelligent people (longer pause) **please be quiet.** (Slightly louder)
> **Lastly** – Young lady/young man, SHUT (pause) UP.

(Soft firm voice directed to the individual still talking.)

Perception and reality

Perception is a conclusion based on observation, understanding, and interpretation. Because people operate at different levels of understanding, perform different levels of observations (from shallow to in-depth), and have different meanings for similar things, events can be perceived differently. These perceptions may be in sharp contrast to what the evidence shows - **reality**.

The advertising industry is based on perception, and it is the leader in distorting reality. Your perception is the basis for buying or supporting a product, service, person, or company. The distortion is present everywhere: in magazines, on billboards, on computers, on the back of doors, in stalls, on television, etc.

You see it, you hear it, you smell it, you taste it, and you touch it. You think it is coconut when it is really syrup and "whatever numbered" flavor. You think it is the king, but it is only beer. You think it is the real thing, but it is mostly sugar and water. The distortion is **so deep**, **so great** that perception becomes reality.

Perception is Real.

♥♥♥♥♥♥♥

I believe that the biggest, most deceptive and immoral practice within society started about 25 years ago – marketing to teenagers. In general, this practice has led to mass marketing and advertising campaigns that are targeted specifically to children. No age is immune.

Children play a role in deciding what products and services are supported in the household. This may seem harmless. OK, on the surface it may be.

Here is a question - *'What happens when your child is given more decision-making authority?'*

Here is the answer. The more decision making authority you give a child, the more the child believes that you have elevated his/her status in the household. Soon, you have a child who believes that he/she is worthy of adult status. *You have elevated your child to an adult.* The roles of the adult and child have become blurred.

Parents, there should always be clear, well-defined, adult-child boundaries.

♥♥♥♥♥♥♥♥

Real case scenario #27
A divorced single mother gives her older son an enormous amount of responsibility and decision-making power. The son is very responsible. He has taken on the male role in the household for the pass three years.

The son is suddenly faced with an intense love affair between his mother and her new lover. The son disapproves of the relationship. He airs his disagreement. He refuses to do several chores, and the lover strikes the boy as a disciplinary action.

The son becomes disobedient and disrespectful to the mother. He resents his mother's lover. His grades begin to decline.

♥♥♥♥♥♥♥♥

Children are not the only ones captivated by perception. Perception can often cloud the judgment of parents.

Real case scenario #28

A father only wants the best for his daughter. He showers her with expensive items at the expense of working long hours and being overextended. At age three, the daughter gets a motorized toy car. At age eleven, she receives name brand clothing costing more than one thousand dollars. For her high school graduation present, she gets a brand new, luxury SUV.

The daughter, a very materialistic young lady, falls in love with a guy who gives her the world. He dresses well. He drives an expensive car. He's handsome. He's debonair and has a MBA from an Ivy League School.

The mother perceives him to be a great catch. She tells her daughter, "That's how your father got me to marry him. He showered me with gifts." They smile at each other.

The young lady and young man get married; she's 22 and he's 27. Two years later, the parents receive a visit from the police. Extensive dialogue occurs between the parents and detectives. The parents are informed that their daughter had committed suicide.

The son-in-law informs the parents that about six months into the marriage, he and his wife started having financial difficulties. He confesses, "I lost my job and had to file for bankruptcy protection. I started working for a salary that would not support our luxurious lifestyle. At that time, Taylor (the daughter) became progressively depressed, drinking and taking prescription drugs. She constantly spoke of being embarrassed and humiliated, especially after the Jaguar was repossessed."

The suicide note reads:

Dear parents:
I know I have let you down. I'm sorry.
Love,
Your little girl

A year after the daughter's death, the parents learned that their former son-in-law lost his original job after being convicted for embezzling funds. Their son-in-law's support for a prostitute and an 18-month-old child, borne outside of the marriage, attributed to the financial hardship. The daughter killed herself after the husband told her about the affair and having contracted AIDS.

Sadly, perception can be deadly.

♥♥♥♥♥♥♥

Life altering consequences can result from the actions of parents and children due to their inaccurate perceptions of reality.

In perception:

- Teenage girls become single parents because they once perceived that sex would result in everlasting love, monogamy, or marriage.
- Parents are failing to recognize their children's substance abuse, because their children have good grades.
- Daughters are being abused by boyfriends who their fathers believe are nice guys.

In reality:

- Giving your kids extravagant materialistic things does not create a child with a high degree of character, integrity, or good grades.
- Being smart or intelligent does not guarantee success.
- Dating members of the opposite sex does not mean your child is a heterosexual. Your child may be dealing with sexual identity issues. He/she may require professional counseling to prevent suicide or substance abuse.
- The abusive unmarried parent is the same abusive married parent.
- Neglected kids, even when caused by an act of love (working to meet needs), can feel lonely, abandoned, or act out.

Parents, teach your child 'how to' distinguish between perception and reality.

♥♥♥♥♥♥♥♥

Parents, I believe that one of the best marketing efforts to camouflage reality is the '**KEEP IT REAL**' campaign. The KEEP IT REAL campaign has led to, as my brother so profoundly puts it, IGNORANCE BEING A FAD.

The more one uses incorrect English , the more '*this is me inappropriate attire*' one wears to a job interview, the more disrespectful one is to another, the more courses one is failing and must pay to take summer courses that were free during the regular school year, the more one easily kills another getting a life sentence without parole, the more criticizing one can be in humiliating another, the more one can be down by referring to one's self as a 'Nigger' (a word used to degrade people), the more one dresses provocatively (which tends to initiate sexually explicit conduct or conversation), the more one deems himself to live in a GHETTO (which is a racial term and has no historical origin in America or referring to Blacks), the more one thinks one knows more than one's teacher, the more one disrespects women, the more one refuses to vote, the more girls refer to themselves as B_ _ _ _ES (female dogs) and whores (females who engage in sex with anyone), the more one can pay young ladies to exploit themselves and then say, "I wouldn't marry that w _ _ _ _", and the more one can shame one's parents (who are providing for one) in public by referring to them by some other name, **THE MORE ONE IS SAID TO BE '*KEEPING IT REAL*'**.

The following behaviors will help to eliminate this perpetuation of ignorance.

1. Protect your child's exposure to ignorance in the home by *blocking the video channels, prohibiting the playing of violent video games and explicit CDs, not allowing cursing in your presence or in your home, and only allowing your child to post positive images in his/her room.*

2. Every morning, before your child leaves home, tell your child you love him/her, give your child a loving comforting hug or pat on the back, and speak words of encouragement.

3. Show your child the real life styles of the 'Keeping it Real' spokespersons. Get pictures of the multimillion-dollar homes in which many of these entertainers live, which are in areas quite different from what they are preaching. Show their hypocrisy.

4. Discuss marketing practices; tell your children the truth about perception.

5. Explain that entertainment is just that, entertainment. Spider man is just a stunt man, you cannot fly like superman, and reality shows are not real.

The reality is:

- Today is a preparation step for tomorrow.
- One sets the tone for how one wants to be treated based on how one speaks and behaves.
- People will tell you what you want to hear to get what they want.

Parents, take care of and teach your children.

9

Teaching adult responsibility

As a parent, you must help your child transition from childhood to adulthood. Early on, you must set limits and guidelines. At a very early age, you must give your child age appropriate tasks. In your effort to aid your child in becoming a respectful, responsible adult with character and integrity, you will give some responsibilities based on your child's maturity level, and others to help your child mature.

Questions regarding children and maturity vary. However, children as young as 13 years of age are being held accountable to adult statutes as more and more states implement and modify laws. Such legislation requires children to be mature enough to understand the consequences of their actions.

Knowing what to teach, how to teach, and when to teach can be perplexing. There are two strategies that are helpful in giving you direction. They are *'go with the flow'* and *'meet an adult move with an adult responsibility.'*

Go with the flow

Society, the media, and the entertainment industry are very good at giving directions on what to teach and when to teach it.

Here are some examples:

*If you are watching the news and notice that a six-year-old child has been kidnapped, it is time to teach/re-teach your child about strangers and what to do if they are approached by them.

*If you overhear your teenage daughter and her friends talking about how they would like to date a cute boy who you know is disrespectful, rude, and cannot read, it is time to teach self-respect. You may consider taking your daughter to a formal ball, political affair, or to visit a college campus in an attempt to expose your daughter to more appropriate young men, young men who are more apt to succeed in life.

*If your child is a fan of '*The Three Stooges',* you want to teach your child that the show is for entertainment purposes only, and not to go around poking people in the eye, etc.

*You read in the paper that a student was sentenced to ten years in jail for child molestation and statutory rape after having consensual sex. If you allow your 17-year-age son to date a 15-year-age girl, you had better tell him that he could be charged with statutory rape because the girl has not reached the age of consent.

♥♥♥♥♥♥♥

Parents, in keeping your eyes and ears opened, you will gather a vast amount of information on what to teach, when to teach it, and in some cases how to teach it.

o   In pre-kindergarten, my child brought home a permission slip allowing the teacher to teach *'good touch bad touch'*. I remember my thoughts exactly. I used two words to describe what I was thinking, 'Already? Whoa!'

o   Many high schools and colleges are teaching *'no means no'*, in an attempt to educate young people on the responsibilities and consequences of engaging in sex.

o   Many middle and high schools are teaching entrepreneurship and business practices. Some schools are opening and running businesses. Other schools are teaching investment practices and participating in the stock market game.

o   Parents, when society is saying that youths lack respect that is a clue to teach or re-emphasize respect to your child.

Real case scenario #29
A young boy couldn't wait until he turned 14 years-of-age, so he could get a job. After turning fourteen, he went to the mall with his resumé in hand. The politeness in his voice, the respectfulness in his approach, and the appropriateness of his attire made an impression on the manager of the ice cream store.

The manager called and spoke with the boy's father. The manager stated, "I couldn't believe how mannerly and well spoken your son is. Many of the older teenagers are not that skilled in seeking a job."

The boy was hired and worked at the ice-cream shop until he was 16 years-of-age.

At 14-years-of-age, this young man, our son, already exhibited the qualities of respect, responsibility, maturity, character, and integrity. These skills become the attributes of a successful adult. When I speak with youths, I often remind them that success is more of an *ART than a SMART*.

Meet adult moves with adult actions/responsibilities

As discussed earlier, the question of a child's maturity varies. Knowing when a child is ready to accept higher levels of responsibility may be perplexing. There are times when the child answers the question for you, when the child makes an adult move.

How you respond to a situation indicates if an adult move was made. Have you ever said: "this is my house; he's acting like he's grown; no she didn't; or she can get out of here with that attitude?" If so, your child has given you the opportunity to implement an adult response and/or responsibility. It is a chess game.

Real case scenario #30

A mother and father tell their son not to buy hip hop rap music or listen to it in their home. One day, the parents return home early only to hear vulgar language blasting from their son's room.

When the parents inquired about the music, the son stated, "I should be able to buy what I want with my money." The father replied, "That's a grown up statement. So you think you're grown?" The son responded, "Well!"

The parents left the room and returned with a list of necessities the son had to purchase:

☐ *Deodorant*
☐ *Hair cuts ($15.00 every 2 weeks)*
☐ *Transportation ($60.00/month)*
☐ *Parents will give $20.00 allowance for shoes and $15.00 for pants and shirts.*

The child still receives his $20.00 per week allowance. However, those four little necessities reduced his discretionary monthly funds from eighty dollars to nearly zero.

After two months, the young man asked to negotiate a deal. The young man stated that he would abide by the rules. The parents took on the responsibility of paying for two-thirds of the transportation cost. The parents stated to their son, "Sometimes, when you make choices, you can't fully erase their effects."

In this scenario, the parents plan paid off. The system they devised worked.

♥♥♥♥♥♥♥

Quite often, the most self-controlled choice parents must make is to allow the process to take care of itself. When a decision is executed, and the child holds out, you may need to let the effects

191

of the decision run its course. This is especially true when you know it is a good resolution.

Real case scenario #31

A teenage girl who believes she is entitled to more liberties tries to broker a deal with her parents. The girl has been employed for two years. She has bought herself a car, and she has paid her car insurance.

The parents acknowledge her statements but point out that her duties were self-serving. The parents comment that becoming an adult suggests having empathy and consideration for others. The parents state, "Since you got the car, we've had to remind you of chores, and your attitude is inappropriate and unacceptable."

Upset, the girl abruptly leaves the room. Later that day, the child misses curfew; she arrives home two hours late. Tension fills the home. For several months, missed curfews, arguments, yelling matches, door slamming, and name-calling ensue.

The parents decide enough is enough. The father wants to put the child out of the house. The mother suggests giving the child major adult responsibilities. The parents settle on giving the child more adult responsibilities.

The strategy includes giving their daughter a section of the basement, an area that occupies approximately fifteen percent of the total square footage of the home. The daughter, in return, pays fifteen percent of the household expenses and for her basic necessities.

After researching the law, the parents decide to take a legal approach. A curfew, based on a city ordinance, is instituted. Many of the guidelines implemented in the home are based on local statute.

As the parents later state, "This grown-up therapy paid off big time." The parents have extra funds and a more responsible respectful daughter.

♥♥♥♥♥♥♥♥

Parents, teaching your child the skills needed to become a responsible adult is not easy. However, failing to teach your child these skills is detrimental to your child's ability to function in society. Nevertheless, plenty of opportunities expire because parents are so upset when their child is rebellious.

Throwing a child out of the house is easy. You are fed up; you throw the child out as if the child is garbage. That is easy. As a parent, your job is not to do what is easy, mindless, or quick. You are given the responsibility to mold and create a respectful, responsible adult with character and integrity - a person who has something to contribute to this world.

Serving the homeless, building houses, and participating in scared straight programs are very helpful tools in teaching empathy and adult consequences. Look for such programs and resources in your area to help you teach your child adult responsibility.

Meet ignorance with adult behavior
Because of today's media blitz, children often mistake ignorant behavior as adult behavior. For example, mocking and the degrading treatment of others are both viewed as grown-up perks. These acts do not represent grown-up behavior, but rather pure ignorance. Adult behavior is conscientious of the consequences of actions. Adult behavior recognizes self-responsibility. Adult behavior teaches and is empathetic to others. Adult behavior is always up-

193

lifting. Adult behavior should recognize *'home court advantage'*.

Real case scenario #32

On a family outing to the museum, my son requested the keys to the car. He claimed that he had been to the museum many times and was bored. I denied the request. Next, my son mocked me and walked away. (I recognized that this was a test.)

I waited until we arrived home, and I told my husband, "I got this." I went into my son's room and verbally drilled into him.

> *I told him that mocking and degrading people are easy; I thought I raised him better than that. I continued speaking, "You are too unique and too intelligent to resort to such low grade behavior. What did you prove? Did you prove you could back talk? Wow! That really is amazing. You proved absolutely nothing. You didn't prove that you could negotiate a deal. You didn't prove that you could look beyond the appearance of things and make the best out of a situation you didn't like. You didn't prove that you could be open-minded. You basically demonstrated a lack of maturity and made me realize that I've given you a lot of unearned credit.*

> *You know, I'm somewhat disappointed. I know you are smarter than what you recently demonstrated. Here you are an 'A' student with nearly 1300 on the SAT (maximum score*

1600), and scholarships at hand, and yet you act like that. That's not how someone with your credentials and potential acts. That's unacceptable, and that's unintelligent."

I continued, "Did you think I would allow you to talk to me like that? What were you thinking? Did you think I would act ignorant when you act ignorant? No. If I had acted like that, you would think that's how people should act, and it's not.

I will tell you this, you will not talk to me any type of way. I can lovingly make your life hard. First of all, the only thing that requires electricity in this house is the refrigerator. I will disconnect everything. You will have the basics while everybody else will have better.

You see, I have plenty of time to teach you a lesson, and I will..."

I continued with this pattern of reaffirming his uniqueness and telling him the truth about his behavior. After lecturing, we began teaching him a lesson that he would never forget, a lesson on the difference between appropriate adult behavior and ignorant behavior.

Parents, I waited until we got home. I waited for home court advantage (a secret I learned from my mother). My son could not go anywhere. He was a captive audience. Every time my son played a regular card, we played a trump card. When he made an adult move, we met it with an adult responsibility and/or consequence. It took a month to break him (as my mother would say) of his misunderstanding of adult behavior.

Parents, ignorant behavior is not adult behavior. Littering, cursing out people , fighting, using and taking advantage of people, not taking care of your responsibilities, not taking care of your children, not working (and being able to work), and verbally, physically, and emotionally abusing people are <u>all</u> ignorant behaviors. These actions do not contribute to being a responsible adult with integrity and character.

Parents, you must teach your child adult behavior and refrain from teaching or demonstrating ignorant behavior.

♥♥♥♥♥♥♥

Today is preparation for tomorrow

Today's child is tomorrow's adult. Today, your child must make steps towards tomorrow.

How is your child preparing for tomorrow, today?

If your child needs a scholarship for college then your child needs a B+ average or above, and a very high SAT score. Time spent volunteering, skill building, engaging in enrichment programs, establishing goal related time lines, and creating step-by-step guides are things your child can do today to help prepare for tomorrow.

♥♥♥♥♥♥♥

'Yin-yang' and *'conflict-ease'* are metaphors that symbolize ideas about negative-positive energy cycles. These cycles reflect the need to prepare for success. During times of yang/ease (positive energy flow) one must prepare for yin/conflict (negative energy flow). Recognizing this strategy allows one to be prepared during the most difficult times of his/her life, and to maneuver through such times, successfully.

Preparations for college, career, family, buying a home, entrepreneurship, and success start today. Steps towards future financial stability should be taken today. Read books that teach you how to save and build wealth. Some books start with simple saving methods, such as saving fifteen dollars a week.

I do not believe in creating chaos. Life will present challenges of its own. There is no need to create drama. The goal is to be ready for the challenges, the unforeseen circumstances, the accidents, and the crises that come in life.

The *'yin and the yang'*, as well as the *'conflict and the ease'* cycles remind us that life is not unbearable when we plan. Parents, this is a concept I strongly recommend that you teach your child.

Groom today's child for tomorrow's adult.

10

Love only sees good

Being a parent does not always have to be stressful. It can be a very loving enjoyable experience. How one goes into parenting dictates the kinds of experiences one will have. A parent who is very optimistic will have more experiences that are positive. A parent who is very pessimistic will have more experiences that are negative.

I have fun in my role as a parent. Getting together with other parents is exciting. The teamwork, the unity, and the support are rewarding. What makes my job most enjoyable is seeing my child grow and develop in 'good'.

Now, there may be deficiencies in your child. Do not fail to acknowledge your child's weaknesses and address them accordingly. Recognizing weaknesses and deficiencies in your child is also **good**. You are in a better position to help your child when you acknowledge your child's weaknesses and deficiencies. However, do not focus solely on them.

As a parent, you want to build from the _good_ of a child. For that reason, you must always see the *good*. You must teach, parent, support, encourage, protect, and nurture from the *good* within your child. A parent must always know that their child has something *good* to offer the world, and must always bring out the *good* in their child. The reason for seeing only _good_ is simple; what you see dictates how you will respond, which influences what you will get.

❤❤❤❤❤❤❤

Perhaps, *'love sees only _good_'* requires a spiritual understanding. Therefore, I have provided scriptures for spiritual guidance.

In Matthew 13: 37-38
> *...He that soweth the good seed is the Son of man.*
> *The field is the world; the good seed are the*
> *children of the kingdom...*

In 3rd John verse 11
> *Beloved, follow not that which is evil, but that which is*
> *Good. He that doeth good is of GOD: but he that doeth*
> *Evil hath not seen GOD.*

Love in itself is a powerful force in the Universe. Having the love that sees only *good* is also powerful. Loving behavior de-escalates violent behavior and resolves conflict. Love builds and nourishes. Love encourages and protects.

In 1ˢᵗ John 4: 7-8

> *Beloved, let us love one another: for love is of GOD; and every one that loveth is born of GOD, and knoweth GOD.*
>
> *He that loveth not, knoweth not GOD; for GOD is love.*

In Proverbs 10: 11

> *Hatred stirreth up strifes: but love covereth all sins.*

Love builds from the good

Loving behavior <u>does not</u> degrade or abuse. There is nothing loving about degradation or abuse. Parents, stop allowing these actions in your household.

Even a well-fed dog will become angry and bite the master or the master's family member that has abused, neglected, or mistreated him.

Think.

Physical abuse is easy. Degradation is easy. Both are mindless and spineless actions.

♥♥♥♥♥♥♥

Does an adult want to be lovingly abused by his/her spouse in order to learn a lesson?

Does an adult want to be lovingly degraded or humiliated by his/her spouse in order to learn a lesson?

Think.

Love builds from the *good* of a child. You do not build a good house on a weak foundation. That is unintelligent. If the foundation is weak, you reinforce it and strengthen it. You repair the foundation with good materials. It is illogical to repair a weak foundation with weak materials thinking it will be strong.

The same principle is used with a child. It is unsound to recognize a weakness in a child and to beat that child, humiliate that child, and neglect that child thinking that the child will be able to stand strong as an adult. When a child has weaknesses and deficiencies, you acknowledge them. You reinforce them with *good* solid teachings. You strengthen your child with loving, encouraging words, and you build from the *good*.

Again, you reinforce your child with *good* solid teachings. You strengthen your child with loving, encouraging words, and you build from the *good* of your child.

♥♥♥♥♥♥♥

Spiritually speaking, Jesus brought us teachings and a better understanding of GOD.

In Luke 4: 4
> ....*That man shall not live by bread alone, but by every word of GOD.*

In Matthew 7: 17-18 it is stated:
> *Even so every good tree bringeth forth good fruit; but a corrupt tree bringeth forth evil fruit.*
> *A good tree cannot bring forth evil fruit, neither can a corrupt tree bring forth good fruit.*

In Luke 11: 10-13

> *For every one that asketh receiveth; and he that seeketh findeth; and to him that knocketh it shall be opened.*
>
> *If a son shall ask bread of any of you that is a Father, will he give him a stone? Or if he ask a Fish, will he for a fish give him a serpent?*
>
> *Or if he shall ask an egg, will he offer him a scorpion?*
>
> *If ye then, being evil, know how to give good gifts unto your children, how much more shall your Father which is in heaven give good things to them that ask him?*

Loving parents take your child, nurture your child, support your child, teach your child, encourage your child, love your child, protect your child, and see the _good_ in your child.

♥♥♥♥♥♥♥

Love overcomes envy

Parents, many times I have been in a state of disbelief when I have come across parents who were jealous of their children. What made it worse was when I could see the greatness, the potential, and the light the child possessed. I truly have been bamboozled, and unable to understand why parents were spiteful, why parents would act this way.

Parents, this is your child. This is the parent of your grandchild. This child will leave a legacy, be it biological or not. Even if this child becomes a stepparent, he/she will influence another child, and the legacy will continue.

Parents, educators are motivating and building the character of children all over the world. Teachers write lesson plans on methods to motivate and build character. It is heart breaking for a child to go home and be told '*you ain't s_ _ _, I ain't s_ _ _ and you ain't going to be s_ _ _, or 'My parents didn't support me; why should I support you?'*

Mothers being jealous of daughters and fathers being jealous of sons are emotions that have no place in the rearing of a child.

Real case scenario #33

In 1971, a couple, in love, marries. The couple has four children. In 1984, the couple divorce, citing irreconcilable differences.

The youngest child decides to embark upon an athletic career. His extraordinary physical talent is inherited from his father. The son earns an athletic scholarship to college. The son is drafted to play for the NHL.

The father is interviewed and wished the best for his son. The father never has seen his son play hockey. The father stated, "I don't want him to focus on the past. You can't change it. I never had a father around..."

♥♥♥♥♥♥♥

Is '*just because you didn't have*' a reason not to give to your child? Is it a reason not to be a mother or father to your child?

Is it a reason for irresponsibly abandoning your child?

It is obvious that on the outside this child is doing well. The question is, '*What is going on with the other three children?*' Here is the answer. *One of the children is in the military service. The second child is in rehabilitation for alcohol abuse. Sadly, the third child was killed in an automobile accident.*

James 3: 16
> *For where envying and strife is, there is confusion and every evil work.*

Parents, you must help your child reach his/her full potential. Take time to nurture your child, support your child, teach your child, encourage your child, love your child, protect your child, and see the good in your child.

♥♥♥♥♥♥♥

Love sees no decision

The decision to take drugs was yours. The decision to have sex with that particular person was yours. The decision to marry was yours. The decision to divorce was yours. The decision to be an alcoholic was yours. The decisions to fornicate, adulterate, steal, lie, murder, become a junkie, be with a man or a woman, have self-pity, to buy a house you could not afford, have kids, or be self-destructive were <u>all</u> yours.

So parents, why do you make your child pay for your decisions?

Real case scenario #34

A girl is raised by her paternal grandmother. The mother left the girl with the grandmother after she and the father ended their relationship. The mother had very few funds to raise a child on her own. Therefore, she decided it would be best to let the grandmother raise her.

The mother went back home to live with her parents. They told her that she could come back home but not with her child.

The mother is White and the father is Black.

Why would the mother's parents not allow their grandchild in their home?

♥♥♥♥♥♥♥

When I was a little girl, I would ask my mother questions like, *"Was it because they were Black?"* My mother would say, *"No, it was because the others have hate in their heart."*

Many people will use hate, disappointment, jealousy, tradition, culture, and religion as a reason to mistreat or not to love children. Parents, do not allow others to mistreat or de-value your child with words, actions, customs, religion, traditions, habits, or beliefs.

Parents, nurture your child, support your child, teach your child, encourage your child, love your child, protect your child, and see the _good_ in your child.

♥♥♥♥♥♥♥♥

Love sees only love
Children do not come into this world bad, ugly, big headed, or committing sins. They come into this world as open, loving individuals.

Children do not come into this world black, white, brown, or yellow. They come into this world as open, loving individuals.

Children do not come into this world short, tall, diseased, or deformed. They come into this world as open, loving individuals.

Parents, you cannot see your child as: the daughter of the guy who dumped me, the son of the woman who cheated on me, the son of the man who hit me, or the daughter of the woman who gave me AIDS.

CHILDREN COME INTO THIS WORLD AS OPEN, LOVING INDIVIDUALS.

Parents, nurture your child, support your child, teach your child, encourage your child, love your child, protect your child, and see only the _good_ in your child.

Parents, <u>You</u> are the Power behind your Child's Success

Psalm 115

Psalm 115

> *Not unto us O Lord, not unto us, but unto thy name give*
> *glory, for thy mercy, and for thy truth's sake.*
>> *Wherefore should the heathen say, where is now*
>> *their God?*
>> *But our God is in the heavens: he hath done*
>> *whatsoever he hath pleased.*
>> *Their idols are silver and gold, the work of*
>> *men's hands.*
>> *They have mouths, but they speak not: eyes have*
>> *they, but they see not:*
>> *They have ears, but they hear not: noses have*
>> *they, but they smell not:*
>> *They have hands, but they handle not: feet they*
>> *have, but they walk not: neither speak*
>> *they through their throat.*
>> *They that make them are like unto them; so is*
>> *every one that trusteth in them.*
>> *O Israel, trust thou in the Lord: he is their help*
>> *and their shield.*
>> *O house of Aaron, trust in the Lord: he is their*
>> *help and their shield.*

Ye that fear the Lord, trust in the Lord: he is
their help and their shield.

The Lord hath been mindful of us: he will bless
us; he will bless the house
of Israel; he will bless the house of
Aaron.

He will bless them that fear the Lord **both** *small*
and great.

The Lord shall increase you more and more, you
and your children.

Ye are blessed of the Lord which made heaven
and earth.

The heaven, even the heavens, are the Lord's:
but the earth hath he given to the
children of men.

The dead praise not the Lord, neither any that go
down into silence.

But we will bless the Lord from this time forth
and for evermore. Praise the Lord.

Nurturance Poem
Author: Phyllis Austin

NURTURANCE POEM

I see the good in my child.
That is the way it should be.
I build on the GOOD,
not the negativity.

When my child moves on
to the adult stage,
I thank God for my child .
I nurtured him the right way.

Daily Affirmations for the Student

Author: Phyllis Austin

Daily Affirmations for the Student
Author: Phyllis Austin

1. I will start in order to finish.
2. I will plan my work and work my plan.
3. I will create and seize opportunities to improve my life.
4. I accomplish all I want to do today with grace, love, and enthusiasm.
5. I believe that I can make it; I will keep on trying.
6. I choose thoughts and words that support and enable me to create the life I really want.
7. I will speak with and talk to others, the way I want them to speak with and talk to me.
8. I will set goals and visualize myself reaching my goals.
9. I will uplift myself when I speak.
10. The harder I work, the easier the work becomes.
11. Daily, I will make and take paths to my goal.
12. I will act and treat myself the way I want others to act towards and treat me.
13. I will stay away from people and places where trouble exists.
14. I will protect my mind from negative and depressive talk.
15. I will be successful, for success is the best revenge. (Think about your high school reunion).
16. I will not give up my power; I will not give up my control. (Good for when others want to make you angry or make you lose control)
17. I will choose greatness.
18. There is only one of me. I am a unique individual; I am special in every way.
19. Whatever I desire, is possible.
20. I have the power to make the changes that I need to make in my life.
21. I will not accept others low expectations of me, as those of my own.

22. I set and live up to my high expectations of me.
23. I will control my destiny.
24. I will not leave my life up to chance.
25. I have the power to write my life and edit my story.
26. I will seek knowledge, wisdom, and discernment.
27. I will go for my dreams. I will make my dreams a reality.
28. I am fully in charge of my own happiness.
29. I am my own best friend-the person I enjoy being with the most. (Good for when you feel lonely)
30. I am confident. I am victorious. I am a winner.
31. I am a beautiful/handsome person.
32. This challenge is only a temporary step in my reality, it is not my reality. I am thankful for the lessons I am learning.
33. I will protect my mind and my body.
34. I will not be a waste dump for other people's garbage, talk, and problems.
35. I will not judge people unless I have walked in their shoes.
36. Today, is the first day of the rest of my life.
37. I love you, but I love myself more. (Very useful when being pressured to have sex to prove love)
38. I am the only one who can accept and place boundaries on me.
39. I move beyond all limitations into a no-limit world. I achieve my goals with ease.
40. **I will not give up on myself. Every day, and in every way, I will make my life better and better.**

Parents, <u>You</u> are the Power behind your Child's Success

To start or locate a
*'**Parents the Power**' Support Group*
in your area, visit
www.parentsthepower.com

FROM **PARENT** TO **POWER**